THE BEST DEVOTIONS OF

Luci Swindoll

WOMENofFAITH™

THE BEST DEVOTIONS OF

Luci Swindoll

ZONDERVAN™

GRAND RAPIDS, MICHIGAN 49530

ZONDERVAN™

The Best Devotions of Luci Swindoll
Copyright © 2001 by Luci Swindoll

Requests for information should be addressed to:

Zondervan, *Grand Rapids, Michigan 49530*

Library of Congress Cataloging-in-Publication Data

Swindoll, Luci, 1932–
    The best devotions of Luci Swindoll/Luci Swindoll.
        p. cm.
    ISBN: 0-310-24177-4
        1. Christian women—Prayer-books and devotions—English.
I. Title.
BV4844 .S95 2001
242—dc21   2001026747

Published in association with the literary agency of Alive Communications, Inc., 7680 Goddard Street, Suite 200, Colorado Springs, CO 80920.

Interior design by Beth Shagene

Printed in the United States of America

01 02 03 04 05 06 07 08 /❖ DC/ 10 9 8 7 6 5 4 3 2 1

My favorite time during a Women of Faith weekend is Friday night, just prior to the conference. The team meets for devotions and prayer with our intercessor, Lana Bateman. With deep appreciation, I dedicate this book to her, whose prayers sustain, encourage, and comfort me time and again. Thank you, Lana.

Contents

Foreword by Sheila Walsh

First Impressions

I remember the first time I met Luci Swindoll. She was sitting at a conference table and laughing with her friend Marilyn Meberg. That was to become a familiar sight. Luci loves to laugh and she loves her friends. She views life as a grand adventure and approaches it with infectious enthusiasm. I have traveled all over the world to places I have never been through her captivating story telling and her wonderful photographs.

You Said What?

I have learned to my cost never to say to Luci, "I'll give you fifty bucks if you fit the word, 'ferret,' into your next television interview." She will find a way to fit it, not once but several times.

Luci also dispenses unusual words of wisdom when you least expect it. We were spending an evening together at a church, sharing the vision of Women of Faith. During a question and answer session, one dear unsuspecting lady asked for any advice that we could pass on. While I produced something fairly boring and predictable, Luci told her, "Don't ever fry bacon in the nude." How eminently practical she is! Just think of all the accidents that will be averted because of that one night!

The Gift-Giver

Luci gives wonderful gifts; however, it always takes me some time to open them. I can't bear to destroy the work of art that is the wrapping! I usually photograph Luci's presents before I open them in vain hope that the next time I wrap a gift I can move away from giving the impression that mine was wrapped by a blind, one-armed squirrel with Parkinson's disease.

Sitting in a basket in my kitchen is a little bag of herbs that Luci brought back from France. In my lingerie drawer there's a beautiful bag of lavender she bought in Provance. On my desk in my office I keep a plate she gave me. It says, "You will gain much wisdom and be very tired." Sometimes when I am very tired, I look at it and smile. I think of Luci and thank God that she is in my life.

A Child's Heart

Luci has great wisdom and the heart of a child. She celebrates the beauty around her. She treasures small wonders and grand surprises. She has taught me to make a party of every day, to look for moments to laugh, to be kind, to be present in this moment. She is not afraid to try something new or to fail; she enjoys the process as much as the destination. She loves to laugh. When Luci laughs I defy anyone to resist joining in whether you know what she is laughing at or not.

That Voice!

Luci has a very distinctive voice. Its deep timbre has a warmth and resonance that makes you want to pull your chair in closer and listen. Her singing voice is like a layer of velvet that other lighter voices can rest upon. She sings and speaks with conviction backed up by a life-time of walking in the same direction. My son, who is four years old, loves to listen to Luci. His eyes become like saucers when she tells a story, and he laughs from the bottom of his soul when she tells a joke.

Luci

There is so much that I could say about Luci Swindoll. If you have never read her writings then I envy this first discovery that is about to be yours. You will laugh and cry. You will stop often and think. Then you will make some changes in your life that you will keep forever. You will be invited to take your eyes off the things that are missing from your life and dance for pure joy at all that is there. She has left indelible fingerprints in my soul, and I am a better woman because she is my friend

"He who loves a pure heart and whose speech is gracious will have the king for his friend" (Prov. 22:11). Luci is loved, not only by the King of Kings but also by all who know her.

Your adventure is about to begin!

Guidance Out of Nowhere

When I am afraid, I will trust in you.
PSALM 56:3

A dear friend of mine who teaches elementary school music got a timely reminder recently of how much simpler life can be when God is in the picture. One Monday afternoon she was feeling apprehensive about having to change the date for a musical program on the school calendar. It meant she had to face the principal, ask for the change, and possibly have her request rejected. As you may know, one can't just arbitrarily switch the dates of the orchestra concert and the big basketball game, for example. These events are determined months in advance and are generally set in concrete!

As she busied herself in her classroom, she rehearsed what she would say to the principal. The fear began to rise in her so much that her anxiety was out of proportion to her upcoming request. She had that "fretful" feeling.

While dusting off her desk, she swept a small scrap of paper to the floor. When she picked it up, she was amazed to read the words, "When I am afraid, I will trust in you." She could hardly believe her eyes; it was just the encouragement she needed to accomplish the task at hand.

She smiled to herself, took a deep breath, and walked straight to the principal's office for her talk. Everything worked out beautifully, and the date was changed on the calendar with only minor adjustments.

Several days later, a little girl in one of her music classes came up to her and whispered, "Mrs. Jacobs, have you by any chance seen a piece of paper with the words, 'When I am afraid, I will trust in you' written on it?" My friend told the child she had seen that paper and it was at her desk.

"Is it yours, Rachel?" The child told her it was. Wanting to make the most of the moment, my friend asked, "Are you all right, honey? How did you happen to have that piece of paper in the first place? Is there anything I can help you with?"

Rachel confided, "Well, remember a few days ago when we had to take all those tests? I was afraid I couldn't pass, so my mom put that note in my lunch box that day, and it really helped me. Then somehow I lost it."

My friend then explained how the child's loss was her gain. She expressed that she too had feared something, found the paper on the floor, and was reminded to face and overcome that fear by trusting God. The very thing that had calmed the heart of the little child was the same thing that calmed the heart of the wise and mature schoolteacher.

Fear is indiscriminate. It affects all of us regardless of our age or position in life. Whether our fear is absolutely realistic or out of proportion in our minds, our greatest refuge is Jesus Christ.

You may wonder how to find that refuge. It is really very simple: As you walk through your days, you encounter various situations in life that trouble you. If you're like me there are decisions that must be made that seem bigger than I have the capacity to handle. Or there's a relationship in my life that's out of whack and needs attention. Perhaps it's a money problem or a doctor's dreaded report that has me upset.

At times like these we can either quiver in our boots and become paralyzed by that "deer caught in the headlights" phenomenon; we can retreat completely, convincing ourselves that the problem doesn't exist; or we can talk to the One who is able to calm our apprehensions and fears and give us courage to move ahead with a heart of confidence and assurance. In other words, we can pray.

There are times you might be so fearful that all you can say is, "Lord, I'm scared. Please give me peace because I'm placing my trust in you. I know you can meet me right here. Please do!" And he will. He will enter into your mind and calm you with his presence.

God wants us to know that he is with us; he is for us. That's why he has given us this verse. Write it out on a piece of paper today and tuck it in your purse as a reminder that he is greater than your fear.

What a blessing it is, Lord, to know you are my strength and my confidence. I am so glad I don't have to depend on myself at this moment. Give me the comfort I need from you to meet my fear head-on, knowing full well that I am completely safe when I put my trust in you. Amen.

It's Later Than You Think

What I mean . . . is that the time is short. . . .
For this world in its present form is passing away.
1 CORINTHIANS 7:29, 31

Funny thing about *time:* Every one of us knows we
have only twenty-four hours a day, yet we try our best
to think of ways to make each day last longer or become
shorter to suit our preferences. While the clock ticks out
the same number of minutes at the same rate every day,
we try to *save* them like pennies in a jar, so we can spend
them someday somewhere else, whenever we choose.

Not a bad idea, but it just doesn't work that way. Many
of us cannot grasp the truth that the time allotted to us on
this earth is sufficient for all the Lord has planned for us
to do. We don't need one minute more or one minute less
to get the job done: the job of *living.*

When I was a child, our family had a chiming clock
that had been handed down through the generations and
was a well-loved treasure. On the hour, of course, it would
chime out the time, and by it we kept on schedule with
meals and departures and awakening and bedtime. Many
nights, from our respective bedrooms, each of us would
call out the number of chimes until the last one stopped.

One night, after we had all gone to bed about mid-
night, the clock began to gong and we started our audible
ritual: "Nine . . . ten . . . eleven . . . twelve." Just as we

closed our mouths after shouting out TWELVE! the clock struck thirteen. We could hardly believe our ears. *Where did that come from?* I wondered, as we all laughed heartily from our beds. Then, almost in perfect unison, we called out: "It's later than you think!"

For most of us, that's the problem: Our greatest fear is running out of time. So we hurry through life trying desperately to get everything done: working overtime, eating fast food in the car, racing down the freeway. We've gone from *The One Minute Manager* to *The One Minute Mother* to *One Minute Wisdom*. Life itself encourages us to hurry. I can do my laundry twice as fast as my grandmother did; I can travel coast to coast faster than my father ever could; I can handle correspondence that took my mother hours with a few keystrokes and mouse clicks. And yet, I seem to have less time than they did. *What has happened?*

In our quest to save time, we're losing something. I thought the other day about how my grandparents valued time. They always had time for my parents and my brothers and me; they had time for music in their home (each of them was a competent musician); they emphasized beautifully served meals, family reunions, and long conversations. It seemed they had time for everything in life that was important, because *they took time to live.* They treasured the biblical injunction that proclaims, "This is the day the LORD has made; let us rejoice and be glad in it" (Ps. 118:24).

Today, this very day, why don't you think of something that takes a bit of extra time to do and *do it*. Do it for yourself. Do it for a family member. Do it for a neighbor or friend. Do it for the Lord. Maybe it will be an act of generosity or a moment of kindness directed toward a loved one or a stranger. Perhaps it will be simply singing a hymn of praise and thanksgiving because your heart is so full of gratitude.

Don't wait for another time. Rejoice in *this* day and be glad! Tonight, your clock *could* strike thirteen.

Father, give me the grace today to take time. Time to be with you. Time to be with others. Time to enjoy the life you have given me. Help me remember that today is the day you have made. May I rejoice and be glad in it! Amen.

Unexpected Delights

For I am the LORD, your God, who takes hold of your right
hand and says to you, Do not fear; I will help you.
ISAIAH 41:13

On the morning of August 11, 1991, I went to my
friend Mary's home for breakfast. As she was setting
the table, I broke my left leg. I don't usually do this sort
of thing, but I was having such a relaxing time puttering
around on her patio, watering and pruning a few plants.
In my effort to pull a loose branch off a big fern (we are
talkin' *really big* here, folks: the fern that ate L.A.), my
feet flew out from under me and I hit the pavement with
a splat. I could swear I heard the bone break. You don't
want me to describe the sound.

Not knowing the extent of the injury, Mary took me to
the emergency room at a nearby hospital where I was
admitted, x-rayed, and told I had a six-inch break in the
fibula, just above the ankle. (That's the smaller of the two
bones that runs between the knee and the foot.) I was
offered the choice between having no surgery (but wearing a cast from toes to groin for eight to twelve months)
or having a metal plate with six or seven screws surgi-
cally inserted in the break area, which would help me
heal in only four months. I chose the latter option.

Well, what an interesting four months those were!
First of all, my orthopedic surgeon, Dr. Michael Kropf,

turned out to be young, good-looking, gentle, and tremendous fun. Even when he changed my initial cast by sawing it off with a vibrating blade and I got a look at my swollen, bruised leg for the first time, he was very tender. He even permitted me to include Mary, who at my request took pictures of the whole procedure. (She got a little queasy, but I did just fine.)

On the third day after the fall and my release from the hospital, I made a conscious decision about the coming months. I wasn't going to let my broken leg, my cast, or my crutches get in the way of my life. In fact, I wrote in my journal (and I quote), "I'm not going to let this stop me. I'll look at every day as a challenge and watch the Lord make the crooked places straight. He knows my need, and he'll meet me there." And did he ever!

There were numerous occasions during that time of healing when he delighted me with his faithfulness. In spite of my broken leg I went to work every day, to Colorado on vacation, and to Italy for Marilyn's daughter's wedding. I never missed a single speaking engagement in six different states.

The most wild experience, however, was in early December when I flew to Chicago where I was to change planes for the Twin Cities. It was very cold and snowing in Chicago when I was met at my gate by an American Airlines attendant with a wheelchair. When he wheeled me over to board my connecting flight, the word "canceled" was flashing on the screen. "Is this flight to Minneapolis–St. Paul *really* canceled?" I asked in all seriousness.

"Indeed it is, ma'am," he replied. "That airport is shut down, and nobody is flying in there today. Sorry."

I asked to be pushed over to a pay phone, where I called my hostess in Minneapolis to report what had happened. "Oh, Luci," she said, "I called you this morning to tell you not to come, but you had already left. I feel so bad that you made this trip for nothing."

Well, as it turned out, it wasn't for "nothing" after all. When I explained my plight to the guy pushing my wheelchair, he smiled sweetly and asked, "May I take you to lunch? Then we'll get you on a return flight to California. Would that be okay?"

Later that evening, I invited a few friends over for pizza. As we were each discussing the events of our day, they asked sympathetically, "And what did you do today, Luci, being in a wheelchair and all?" I *delighted* in telling them I had flown to Chicago for lunch!

Each of us has something broken in our lives: a broken promise, a broken dream, a broken marriage, a broken heart . . . and we must decide how we're going to deal with our brokenness. We can wallow in self-pity or regret, accomplishing nothing and having no fun or joy in our circumstances; or we can determine with our will to take a few risks, get out of our comfort zone, and see what God will do to bring unexpected delight in our time of need.

Ernest Hemingway puts it this way in *A Farewell to Arms:* "The world breaks everyone and many are strong at the broken places." I challenge you to be one of the many. Take that step of faith and ask God to surprise you in a unique way that only he has the flair to accomplish.

Lift my spirits today, Lord, out of my own dilemma, into the light of your presence and provision. Help me look at life in a fresh, exciting way, different from before, being assured that you do not disappoint. I praise you for what you will do in my life today, and I can't wait to see it happen. Amen.

I Dare You

Do not boast about tomorrow, for you do not know
what a day may bring forth.
PROVERBS 27:1

More often than not I wish I had taken a camera along to capture some of the zany antics of Marilyn and me. Then maybe people would believe they really happened. However, the story I am about to relate is one of those rare occasions that I will be forever grateful no camera was available to record.

I had been living in Southern California for about a year when I received a call from a former Mobil Oil supervisor in Dallas; he was going to be vacationing in my area and would like to take me to dinner. I was thrilled with the prospect. Bill was a man I had dated a few times in Texas, and I always enjoyed his company . . . not to mention his tall, handsome looks and stylish grooming. He was great fun to be with and a gentleman.

During the afternoon of the day Bill and I were to go out, I was riding along in Marilyn's car on the way to my house after we picked up her daughter from school. When I mentioned my *big evening,* she asked what I was planning to wear. "Well, I don't know . . . I really haven't thought about it. What do you think?" She liked the pantsuit I had on and suggested I wear that, but we both noticed a little spot on the front of the jacket; it really needed cleaning before it could be worn again. Marilyn said, "Oh well, you'll find something else, I'm sure," and turned on my street to drop me off.

"Wait a minute, Mar," I said. "Take me to the cleaners. I want to wear *this,* and if I don't get it there right now I can't have one-hour service."

She stopped the car, looked at me, and inquired, "What will you wear home, Luci? You don't *have* to wear that outfit tonight, you know."

"Oh yes, I do. Please . . . just drive me to the cleaners, and I'll take this off in the car and go home in my underwear. You'll take it in for me, won't you, and protect me from being seen?"

Immediately, I began to undress — jacket, blouse, slacks — as Marilyn headed for the cleaners. I hunkered down in my panties and bra while sweet little eleven-year-old Beth just stared at me in horror from the backseat. "Don't worry, honey," I assured her, "your mother won't let me be seen in my underwear. It's all right."

When we got to the cleaners' parking lot, I offered a silent prayer of thanks when I saw there was no one else there. Marilyn took my clothes, opened the door, and *left it wide open* as she proceeded into the cleaners to request one-hour service on my behalf. I scrambled to hide behind my purse, a box of Kleenex, and the steering wheel as another car pulled in and Beth slithered to the floorboard for cover.

When Marilyn got back in the car I choked on a half-hysterical giggle. "Marilyn . . . *how could you* leave that door open? What if a church member had driven up, or somebody who craved my body? What would I have done?"

In mock innocence she said, "I left the door open? How careless of me."

All the way home we laughed ourselves silly: she, from an upright position behind the steering wheel; I, hunched over with my head in my purse; and Beth, muttering from the backseat floorboard, "I don't believe this . . . I just don't believe it."

From inside my house, Marilyn brought me an old beat-up housecoat that I wouldn't wear to dump the garbage, much less in front of my apartment. But what could I do? I threw the robe on and marched up my walkway like that housecoat was what I always wore to pick up Beth from school. Even now, in the recesses of my mind, I can still hear Marilyn's cackling laughter as she sped away, and see Beth's head through the back window, shaking from side to side in perpetual incredulity.

Is there a moral to this crazy story? I think there is — an important one. Some of us are so set in concrete, we can't remember when we last laughed. Or created anything to laugh *at*. Everything is terribly serious. Heavy. Solemn. I'm not saying there's no place for this kind of attitude . . . but *every minute of the day?* Where is the joy? Where is the zaniness?

I dare you to do something today that will make you giggle. Invent it yourself. Bend a little. Dare to embrace something a bit risky and wild. And don't put it off until tomorrow. How do you know tomorrow will ever get here?

Creator of joy, help me this very day to look around and find something to laugh about. Doesn't have to be big. Doesn't have to be unusual. Just some little thing to remind me you are a God of jubilation. Keep me from being a stick-in-the-mud! Help me to have fun today, and not put it off until tomorrow. Amen.

Enough Is Enough

But godliness with contentment is great gain.
For we brought nothing into the world,
and we can take nothing out of it. But if we have food
and clothing, we will be content with that.

1 TIMOTHY 6:6–8

A few years ago a friend was spending the weekend with me, and when we awakened on Saturday morning she asked, "What shall we do today? Where would it be fun to go? The mall? The movies? The museum?" I think she was pretty stunned when I suggested we stay home. "And do *what?*" she questioned. "What about the beach, or the mountains, or the desert? Shouldn't we go someplace? It's Saturday!" She could not imagine staying home on a day we had set aside for fun.

"Well," I said, "why don't we do something here and enjoy what we already have?"

"Oh," she muttered. But she really became intrigued with the idea as I explained how I feel that we sometimes go running around looking for and buying more things—things we might already have. Why don't we just stay home and enjoy them?

That's what my friend and I did that day . . . *and she loved it.* We worked on a jigsaw puzzle, listened to our favorite music, read to each other, played a game, made little meals, all the while having wonderful conversation. We went to bed that night completely satisfied.

Since that day, my friend has said to me many times, "That helped me so much. I've really learned to stay home and enjoy what I already have." Now when she comes here she never wants to leave. If we go to the mall or the movies, it's because I drag her. Not long ago I found a delightful little devotional book, and I couldn't wait to buy it for her. The title? *Staying Home*.

What we learned that day is that enough is enough, even though there are times we're afraid to test it. We're kind of scared that what we have won't be enough to satisfy us.

One day I decided to count all the projects I had in my house (things I could make with my hands), and determine just how long I could go without buying another thing. These might be kits or models, or patterns for designs to be created out of paper, yarn, wood, or clay. When I finished counting, I figured I had *seven years'* worth of projects. I don't even know if I'll live that long!

Why do we so often feel that "there's something better out there"? I believe we're often uncomfortable with ourselves, so we go outside ourselves in search of someone, or something, or some place that will bring us contentment. We want to be somebody else, somewhere else, doing something else, and truthfully, we will settle for almost anything. And what does the Bible say about that? In Philippians 4:11, Paul says it all: "I have learned to be content whatever the circumstances."

If you struggle with discontentment (and we all do sometimes), let me make three simple suggestions that might help:

1. Look around and consider your blessings. Read this morning's newspaper and be grateful for what didn't happen to you. Think about what you do have in a new light. As a single friend of mine says, "I'd rather want what I don't have than have what I don't want."

2. Look around and consider what you already have. Is there music you can hear, books you want to read, projects you want to complete, letters you would enjoy writing, friends you want to call? Do that today, instead of going out "in search of . . ."

3. Look around and consider how far you've come. Remember the days when you didn't know the Lord, when you were at ground zero. Think of how far he's brought you and rejoice in that.

The key to contentment is *to consider*. Consider who you are and be satisfied with that. Consider what you have and be satisfied with that. Consider what God's doing and be satisfied with that. You will be amazed at how much more comfortable you'll feel with yourself.

Finally, consider this: If contentment cannot be found within yourself, you'll never find it.

Lord, make me content with who I am, what I have, and where I find myself. Because it is here, at this point, that you will meet me and, if necessary, change me. Amen.

Make Something with Your Hands

Make it your ambition to lead a quiet life, to mind your own
business and to work with your hands, just as we told you,
so that your daily life may win the respect of outsiders and
so that you will not be dependent on anybody.
1 THESSALONIANS 4:11–12

I can't tell you how much I love that verse! First of all, it
actually says "mind your own business." How many
times have you wanted to say that to someone but
thought it might be un-Christian, so you kept your mouth
shut . . . and here it is, *in the Bible*. (I hasten to add that it
will be wiser if you let the other person find that verse
for herself rather than suggesting she apply it in her life.)

Second, I appreciate any mandate that encourages me
to work with my hands, because I heard that injunction
so often as a child, from my mother. Bored with my little
life, I would go to her in the desperation that only a ten-
year-old can feel and beg her to tell me what to do. "Make
something with your hands," she'd say, then suggest what
that something might be. A greeting card. A painting. A
mask. A little basket out of toothpicks or Popsicle sticks.
A schoolbook cover. She even suggested on one occasion
that I help her make peanut brittle, which ended in utter
disaster. I knew something was wrong when I attempted

to lift the spoon out of the pot full of ingredients and everything came with it: peanuts, brittle, pot, and all. "Maybe we could call this modern art instead of candy?" I queried.

As I grew older, this love of handmade things grew with me. I could never get my fill of anything that permitted me to create or invent something from my own mind and hands and imagination. When I learned that Betsy, a friend from my early days at Mobil Oil, was extremely competent with knitting, I asked her to tell me what all she had made. She mesmerized me with stories of how she used to sit in dark movie houses, watching the film and following the plot, yet all the while knitting up a storm on some sweater or pair of socks she later sold to a little boutique in her hometown of Nashua, New Hampshire. I was amazed at the extent of her prowess.

"Do you think *I* could learn to knit?" I asked one day in complete candor.

"Of course," she replied, "anybody can learn it. It's just the mastering of a skill. What would you like to make?" When I informed her I had always wanted a cashmere coat, she swallowed hard and suggested I might want to start with a pot holder.

"Fine," I agreed, knowing full well I would get the hang of it in no time and by winter would indeed be wearing a coat of my own making.

Well, needless to say, knitting was a lot harder than I had imagined. Without my permission my hands clenched as I knitted and pearled away, and as the yarn tightened I ended up with an item that resembled a hockey puck instead of a pot holder. Betsy tried to encourage me and even offered to take over for me (which prompted my thoughts to go to the "mind your own business" part of the verse I referred to earlier).

Several months down the road, I finally admitted that proficiency in the skill of knitting was not to be. I kept that little hockey puck for years, however, as a reminder of the fun I had during those days of laughing and learning with Betsy. I may not have a cashmere coat, but I have lots of greeting cards, little paintings, masks, and handmade baskets. And I treasure them all.

God invites us to express our uniqueness and have fun by making things with our hands. These things don't have to be big or elaborate or even "correct," but making them should provide solace and personal fulfillment. Handmade things should reflect us: a fine meal, a garden patch, a beautiful quilt, a backdrop for a play, a piece of music, a poem, a letter. The idea is to keep our hands busy with meaningful activity so that we develop inside ourselves, depending upon the Lord and not on others for endorsement or approbation. May God help us to express and define ourselves in our one-of-a-kind way.

Lord, remind me that I don't need the approval of someone else as long as you approve of me. May the way I live my life and the works of my hands reflect your glory and bring praise to you. Amen.

Write It Down

Remember that you were slaves in Egypt
and that the LORD your God brought you out of there
with a mighty hand and an outstretched arm.
DEUTERONOMY 5:15

In the wee hours of my childhood mornings when I would come, sleepy-eyed, from my bedroom, there would be my mother, in prayer or Bible study. That picture of her sitting on her bed is impressed on my mind forever. In one hand she'd have her Bible and in the other, a notebook—or as she called it, "My Promise Book." Mother kept a record in that book of what God was teaching her, people she was praying for, issues she was concerned about, neighbors she wanted to see come to Christ. Every day she journaled her thoughts, feelings, God's promises to her, the words to hymns she found encouraging, poetry, and prayers. Mother's notebooks were a tremendous encouragement to her faith.

Now, many years later, they are an encouragement to me. After Mother's death, I kept her notebooks and, through the years, have referred to them on occasion. I cannot tell you how much they have taught me about her and about life. For example, I found written the fourth stanza of the hymn, "Oh Zion Haste":

Give of thy sons, to bear the message glorious;
Give of thy wealth to speed them on their way;
Pour out thy soul for them in prayer victorious;
And all thy spending Jesus will repay.

My mother wrote that, my mother prayed that, my mother did that. When I look at my brothers, both in lifetime Christian ministry, I realize my mother's impact on them (dare I say, on the world) is immeasurable. And to me, Mother modeled the importance of writing down my thoughts and concerns. I've journaled off and on my whole life, and for eleven years I have journaled *every day.*

My journals chronicle my joys and sorrows, progression and regression, trends, desires, regrets, and promises to myself (some kept, some broken). In various ones I have written prayers, songs, and poetry, and I've drawn pictures or used stickers on many of the pages. As I look back over them from time to time, I'm reminded that I was once "a slave in Egypt" and that God redeemed me and put a new song in my mouth and a spring in my step. He continually extends himself toward me, and I read of that over and over in those now yellowed pages.

There are many benefits to journaling, but for me one stands out above all the rest. I put a premium upon knowing one's self, and the blank pages of a journal give me a place to become better acquainted with me. I can explore my own feelings and questions, or come to grips with my own confusion or angst. I can cry as I write, or laugh. I can sort through my life's experiences and gain understanding about myself. I can privately wrestle with personal issues and conflicts.

None of this is an end in itself. Rather, it is my most effective tool for working through life's experiences and all the matters that concern me. Baring my soul in this manner takes me beyond a superficial, shallow existence or relationship with the Lord. I come to him with my eyes wide open and with understanding about myself. I am completely transparent with what I bring to him; consequently, it makes my relationship with him sweeter and far more intimate. In short, it helps me grow.

If you have never journaled, please don't let all this scare you. Don't be intimidated. Start where you are. Give it a try. Get a notebook. Take some time. See what happens. I think you'll surprise yourself with what comes out of your heart and mind. You don't have to be a "writer"—just let your thoughts, dreams, feelings, and prayers flow from you onto that page in your notebook. Nobody's going to see it but you. Be honest and real. And remember, you're not talking to yourself, but to the One who made you, loves you unconditionally, and receives you blameless.

Lord, I praise you for the way you work in my life. Thank you for giving me the freedom to bare my soul to you anytime, in any way. I am awed by the fact that you want to commune with me, exactly as I am. Give me the courage to always be honest with you. Amen.

A Place for You

In my Father's house are many rooms;
if it were not so, I would have told you.
I am going there to prepare a place for you.
JOHN 14:2

What a promise! Jesus is preparing *a place for me*. My own room. This is really important to me, and here's why: *I have to have a place.*

In my adult life I have moved about ten different times, and in every case I notice a pattern. The first thing I do, long before I unpack everything, is prepare a place for myself. It goes like this: I move the most comfortable chair over to one corner and put a table beside that chair with a radio, lamp, the book I'm reading, and a bouquet of flowers. I hang a painting on the wall behind the chair, enclose it with either a screen or stack of boxes, toss a throw rug on the floor, and count it my haven. There may be chaos in every other corner of the house but not in this one. I have a place to go to escape. Blessed retreat.

When I travel I also notice a pattern. It goes like this: I check into a room, and even if I'm going to be there only one night, I unpack my entire suitcase and put my stuff in the drawers and on the bathroom counter. I put away the luggage and place the little treasures I brought from home strategically around the room: my Bible, my journal, my music, my tiny little leather-bound world atlas . . . all stuff I might need. In short, I prepare a place for myself.

When I board an airplane I again notice a pattern. It goes like this: The minute the FASTEN SEAT BELT sign goes off I open my carry-on bag and take out my stuff. I surround myself with my books, a newspaper, a magazine, a postcard I want to write, and I prepare a little place for me for the duration of the trip. I all but hang a little cross-stitched HOME SWEET HOME sign on the food tray.

Call me eccentric (and many do) but it is my way, and I'm glad to know it's God's way too. *He* is preparing a place for me.

Our "place" provides so much . . . not only shelter but also a setting to be alone or together with those we love. Our place is an expression of who we are. It reflects our inner person.

When the six of us on the Women of Faith team arrive in a city, it's only a matter of time until we all congregate in one of our rooms. This is never planned beforehand, nor orchestrated by anyone, but it always happens. We gravitate to a quiet place to fellowship with one another. You probably do the same thing with your friends. You use your "place" to be with others.

But let me ask you this: Have you discovered the value of being alone in your own place? The author Leo Buscaglia writes, "We all need our separate worlds, apart from others, where we can quietly retire for regrouping, for getting back in touch with ourselves. We need this personal solitary place as a pleasant alternative to our more public lives. We must treasure this part of our existence as much as we do the more social part. Then, when loneliness comes, we will have that special place to fall back upon."

Oh, how true! Jesus himself sets the example. Consider John 6:15, where it says that "Jesus . . . withdrew again to a mountain by himself." In the Old Testament we are instructed by the Lord to "come away, my lover" (Songs 8:14).

Your idea of creating a place to be with yourself may not be the same as mine, and that's fine. But I can promise you that until you learn that solitude is your friend and not your enemy, until you are comfortable "staying in your own orbit," you will have little to give anyone else. Buscaglia says every individual has the "sacred responsibility of becoming a complete person." When that happens, having a place all our own will have its greatest value. In it we can celebrate our uniqueness and rejoice with our Savior.

Jesus, just as you are ultimately preparing a room for me for all eternity, help me to have the wisdom to create a special spot to be with you . . . to be alone . . . to engage in meaningful communion with others. Amen.

This Is Not What I Had in Mind

In his heart a man plans his course,
but the LORD determines his steps.
PROVERBS 16:9

One of the most delightful weekends I had spent since moving to California six months before was nearing an end as two teenage girls approached me while I was counting out my vitamins. "What are all those pills for?" one of them asked. "Well," I explained, "these two are for beautiful eyes, this one is for long willowy legs, that little one is for pearly, white teeth . . ." and as I was waxing on, the other girl interrupted me with, "Haven't been taking them long, have you?"

What a comeback! This girl was one sharp cookie. In fact, all twelve of them were.

The Pioneer Girl retreat had been filled with laughter and hilarity, as well as sweet communion and meaningful interaction. And, to think . . . I almost missed it.

You see, Marilyn had signed me up to join her in teaching a class of Pioneer Girls on Wednesday nights at our church in Fullerton, California. I was not thrilled. I had done this to people but had never had it done to me. I remember signing up a fellow employee at Mobil Oil to play on the baseball team. I even volunteered her to be captain of the team, just to hear her try to worm out of it when the team manager phoned her. But somehow I had escaped this type of unsolicited commitment from my friends — until Marilyn came along.

Now, here I was, a teacher to these young teenage girls, who would look to me for spiritual and emotional guidance on Wednesday evenings. This was the *last* thing in life I wanted to do. I resisted mightily:

1. I'm not qualified . . . I've never taught this kind of class before.
2. I've got better things to do with my time, like watch the Wednesday night TV lineup.
3. I'm too tired after working all day.
4. The pay's too low (after all, I was volunteering).

I could come up with at least ninety-eight reasons why I didn't want to do this. But Marilyn had put my name on the dotted line to teach for a year, no less! I could have died, right after killing her.

But, as is always the case, God knew what I could not have known: that I *needed* this experience. I needed the opportunity to prepare for the Bible studies I would teach those young girls. I found that what I was teaching them was rubbing off on me. I got to know them, their parents, and their siblings. Before I knew it I was investing in their futures as they talked about their schoolwork, their boyfriends, their problems, their fears . . . on and on and on. As long as I would listen, they would talk. About everything. And, as I spent those hours with Marilyn (fairly early in our own relationship), I came to see what a fun, joyful, dear friend she was going to be.

God did several meaningful things in my life during that year, and I'm so glad I taught that class in spite of my initial resistance.

What are you resisting? Has God been nudging you into action and you've either said "no" repeatedly, or "well, maybe" so weakly that no one can hear it? I can tell you from my own experience, the very thing we say "no" to just might be God's blessing in disguise. He wants to bless us; he wants to mature us; he wants to get us out of our comfort zone.

The *last* thing you want to do just might be the best thing that ever happened to you. It might even be fun.

How often I resist your bidding, Lord, and miss opportunities to enjoy your gifts. Because of my fear and insecurity, I hesitate; I look within instead of looking to you. Show me your agenda for today, God, and give me the grace and boldness to follow it. Surprise me with your wisdom and delights. Amen.

The Big Little Word: Let!

He who has an ear, let him hear.
REVELATION 13:9

Last week I was in the grocery store and there was a
mother and her little son in front of me, pushing their
cart along. This kid was driving me crazy with his constant demands: "Let me hold that. Let me push the cart.
Let me ride up there. Let me have the cookies. Let me
see that box. Let me buy that candy. Let me pay the
money." I'm telling you, I was standing there thinking,
Let me at that kid! I wanted to say to that mother, "Why
did you ever teach your son the word *let?* Didn't you
know it would come to this? Don't you know what that
word means?"

Let! That's one of the most powerful words in the English language. It says, "Allow me . . . permit me." It urges
consent. As I drove home from the store, I kept thinking
about that word, and I realized it is used repeatedly in the
Bible. In fact, when I got home, I looked up the number
of times it could be found. Would you believe over nine
hundred? I took time to check out some of the references
and found that the "let verses" cover practically every
mandate in the Christian life. Just listen to a few:

1 John 4:7 — Let us love one another.
Hebrews 12:2 — Let us fix our eyes on Jesus.

Colossians 4:6 — Let your conversation be always full of grace.

Psalm 5:11 — Let all who take refuge in you be glad.

Psalm 95:2 — Let us come before him with thanksgiving.

Psalm 99:1 — Let the nations tremble . . . let the earth shake.

Psalm 119:27 — Let me understand the teaching of your precepts.

Proverbs 1:5 — Let the wise listen and add to their learning.

Proverbs 3:3 — Let love and faithfulness never leave you.

Romans 14:13 — Let us stop passing judgment on one another.

Galatians 6:9 — Let us not become weary in doing good.

Colossians 3:15 — Let the peace of Christ rule in your hearts.

Here are only twelve references, and remember — there are over nine hundred! Choose any one of those and give it your consideration; you could be thinking about it for hours. Let (there's that word again!) me challenge you to do a personal Bible study on this simple, wonderful, powerful word. Look it up in your concordance, write down a reference, look up the verse, meditate on it, and ask God to make it real in your life.

I did that with Galatians 5:25, which says, "Let us keep in step with the Spirit." What does this mean to me today? To keep in step means to allow the Holy Spirit to guide my life. That requires from me a response that says, "Lord, I will go where *you* want me to go, I will do what *you* want me to do, I will be what *you* want me to be, because I trust *you* to keep me in step with you." This puts the responsibility in its proper place: on the shoulders of the Holy Spirit and not on mine. He does the guiding, I do the letting.

I wish I could see that little kid now. I think I would listen to him differently. Instead of seeing him as a nuisance, I might see him as a good reminder of what God wants to say to me: "Luci, *let me . . .*"

Next time you're in the grocery store and would like to throttle some demanding child, let him or her instead serve to remind you that God wants to get your attention. He wants to say to you, *"Let . . ."*

Heavenly Father, give me an ear that can hear you in the simplest ways. As I go about my duties today, help me hear your voice in that of another's so I will let go of my will and direct my attention to yours. Let your light shine upon my path so each step I take will be guided by you. Amen.

Put Away Your Coupons

Woe . . . to those who say, "Let God hurry, let him hasten
his work so we may see it. Let it approach, let the plan
of the Holy One of Israel come, so we may know it."
Isaiah 5:18–19

I have just returned from lunch with Marilyn. We went to our favorite Mexican restaurant in the neighborhood. She wanted a potato taco, and I had the coupon that offers a second meal free. I figured that would be my meal. However, when all was said and done, Marilyn asked me for half the price of her meal, so I forked it over.

Don't you just love coupons? I do. In fact, when I got home from lunch and checked my mailbox, there was another bunch. I went through them hastily to see where I might want to go for dinner. To my delight they offered much more than meals. In fact, I figured I could start using them the next morning and keep myself busy all day.

I could start out with bacon and eggs for breakfast at Le Peep followed by a thigh-lift at The Plastic Surgery Institute. After a sandwich and bowl of soup at Donati's Grill, I'd have my dog groomed at Pet Luv (the deal included a free goldfish—figure that out!) and get a haircut at Family Hair Salon. After relishing a pepperoni-with-double-cheese "Round Table" pizza for dinner, I could top off the day by being cremated at sundown for only $545. (I'm not kidding, there was a coupon I could fill out to get a free brochure on the Cremation Services of the Desert.)

One little envelope held every essential thing for the well-equipped woman. The gamut of choices reminds me of a little sign I once received from Barbara: EAT WELL, STAY FIT, DIE ANYWAY!

On occasion I go to God's Word in search of a "coupon" — something I can tear out and take with me to use for a quick, half-price repair job. I don't really want it to cost me much, but I do want it to provide whatever I need for meeting the demands of that day. I don't have time to linger over the Scripture, so I say, "Lord, give me the short version, the coupon, the easy fix. After all, I've got things to do!" In short, I want God to hurry. But the Bible says woe to those who say, "Let God hurry." He doesn't take shortcuts.

Coupons save time and money. They provide immediate results and less expensive ways to have what we want or need. That's nice. But you know what? In God's economy there are no coupons or discounts. And do you know why? Because we don't need them. Discounts are unnecessary. The apostle Peter tells us, "His divine power has given us everything we need for life and godliness through our knowledge of him who called us by his own glory and goodness" (2 Peter 1:3).

Imagine! He has given us *everything* we need.

Unfortunately, most of us go through life feeling like we're long on need and short on resources. So we look for coupons. We present various offerings to the Lord as if he were some grocery-store clerk: "God, if you'll _____, I'll _____." We offer "coupons" to him and hope he'll redeem them. In the process, we miss the essence of what Peter taught. He assures us that in Christ and through his goodness, you and I have everything we need for life. When Christ redeemed us, he made coupon redemption superfluous.

Are you feeling long on need and short on resources today? Let me encourage you to do what I do when I feel that way: go to the One who has promised to provide everything you need, in abundance. He may not give you the answer you had envisioned, but you can trust it to be the perfect provision. He has promised his fullness. No half remedies. No special deals. So put away your coupons.

Lord Jesus, you know what I need today, even better than I do. You know the longing of my soul and my deepest desire. Only you can fill that need, because you know best. Thank you for promising to fill me with everything I truly need. I rest in you and what you will soon provide. Amen.

Stop Comparing

We do not dare to classify or compare ourselves
with some who commend themselves.
When they measure themselves by themselves and
compare themselves with themselves, they are not wise.

2 Corinthians 10:12

The story of my life can be summed up in three words: *Bookended by Brilliance*.

Growing up in my family had a built-in challenge. My two brothers, by anybody's standards, are exceptional. They were as children, and they are now as adults. Both my older brother, Orville, and my younger brother, Chuck, are extremely accomplished, talented, musical, witty, warm, and loving. My challenge was to believe it was okay to be me without comparing myself to them. No one needed to tell me they were going to be "great" someday; I could sense it even in childhood.

Orville was always in a league of his own. He had his own ideas and dreams. Because he made top-notch grades, Mother and Daddy permitted him to have more privileges at a young age than other parents might have let their own sons have. Orville was an accomplished pianist, a math whiz, and a scholar. Not only that, but he was also an obedient son and attentive brother. He wasn't perfect, of course, but pretty close. My problem was that I wanted to be just like him.

Chuck, while quite different from Orville in temperament, was equally gifted and outstanding. Coupled with academic gifts was (and is) a tremendous sense of humor. He loves to laugh and has the ability to make everybody else laugh as well. Chuck and I were great pals as children, often pitting ourselves against the king of our immediate universe, Orville. We stood by each other and defended one another from Orville's lofty ambitions for which he wanted to engage us as slaves. In this competitive arena, I wanted to be just like Chuck.

Looking back now from fifty-plus years out, the saving grace in our family was that on the deepest level each of the siblings liked each other. We were proud of each other. And our parents didn't compare us to each other. They were far more interested in the development of our character than in our appearance or performance. In fact, if I remember correctly, our parents focused on where we were, who we were with, what we did, when we got home, and how we behaved. They emphasized learning, patriotism, family loyalty, and faith, and I believe they really sought to strike a balance in our home.

Even so, I compared myself with my brothers. Why? I don't know. No one had to spend time teaching me that; I managed it quite well on my own. It seems to be part of human proclivity, does it not? I've heard Chuck say numerous times in sermons: "Know yourself, like yourself, be yourself." For a great part of my life I've had to work toward the truth that it's *okay* to be me.

When Scripture teaches that it is not wise to measure or compare ourselves with others, I think we should pay attention. When we compare, we almost always come up short. Or, perhaps worse, we decide we're better than someone else. Either way, it causes stress.

If you're not happy with who you are, you'll spend precious energy trying to be somebody you're not, and it will wear you out. Think for a moment. Is there anybody in your life you're comparing yourself to? A beautiful sister? An accomplished brother? A friend who never seems to have problems? A sports figure who excels with little effort? Well, may I say with all the love in the world: *Quit it.* That business of comparing is going to make you sick and unproductive, if it hasn't already. You are you. God made you, you. And you are exactly who he wants you to be. Don't be somebody's clone. That person you're trying to be may very well be trying to be you.

Let's just all relax and be *ourselves*. It's so much easier. And a lot more fun.

Lord, what a wonderful feeling it is that I don't have to be someone else ... and they don't have to be me. You have called us each to be ourselves. Help me find the joy today in being me. Amen.

Epitaphs

Give her the reward she has earned,
and let her works bring her praise at the city gate.
PROVERBS 31:31

As an art major in college, I often painted outdoors. Laden with easel, paints, brushes, water can, and camp stool I would strike out to wherever the flowers were prettiest. More often than not that led me to the local cemetery. It was delightful being outside in the sunshine, and I was always intrigued with the headstones on various graves: the bas relief carved in cement, the words that supposedly reflected the person whose bones rested there. To me it was all very fascinating.

As the semester progressed I found I was as interested in the epitaphs on the tombstones as I was in the flowers that bloomed throughout the cemetery. I stooped down to read many of them and found it remarkable that a few short words could sometimes capture the entire essence of a person.

It is my understanding that W. C. Fields, for example, had etched on his tombstone, "On the whole, I'd rather be in Philadelphia." And how about the woman who had her potato salad recipe carved into her headstone. Apparently, during her lifetime everybody wanted that recipe and her response was always: *"Over my dead body."* I have a close friend who never gets quite as much sympathy as she likes when she's feeling bad, so she wants to be remembered by these loving words: *"See, I told you I was sick."*

Most of us won't have the prerogative to write our own epitaph. It will be written by someone else . . . someone who will seek to capture a single phrase epitomizing our entire life. If you were to die today, what phrase captures your essence? What words characterize you?

In a sense, we are writing our epitaph every day. What would yours say today? I know people who are so rich in character that there are not enough words in the English language to describe the beauty and outreach of their life, much less to reduce that life to a single phrase. On the other hand, I know folks whose cantankerous spirit leaves one searching for something . . . anything . . . that can summarize their life kindly.

For some of us, the message on our tombstone seems like something in the far-distant future. However, we never know. (Reminds me of a friend who told me she's used up so many sick days, she's going to have to phone in *dead.*) James 4:14 tells us, "Why, you do not even know what will happen tomorrow. What is your life? You are a mist that appears for a little while and then vanishes."

Picture that in your mind's eye. A vanishing vapor, *poof!* What could be more uncertain?

The Creator has made us each one of a kind. There is nobody else exactly like us, and there never will be. Each of us is his special creation and is alive for a distinctive purpose. Because of this, the person we are, and the contribution we make by being that very person, are vitally important to God.

That makes me want to be *today* exactly who God made me, and no one else. This may be the last day I have.

Father, thank you that you designed me uniquely. You've gifted me uniquely, and you have a unique plan for me. Show me that plan today, and give me the grace and courage to live it out with gusto. Amen.

The Greeks Have Stolen My Heart

As you sent me into the world,
I have sent them into the world.
JOHN 17:18

Opposites attract, so they say. And I think they're right.

For more than twenty-five years I have been close friends with a Greek family who lives in Athens. From all outward experience, we have little in common. We don't think in the same language, live in the same country, share the same culture, or embrace the same political values. Perhaps most significantly, we do not have the same philosophy of life. Nevertheless, our friendship has grown and blossomed. That's because we've found common ground in matters of the heart. We love each other.

The first Stylianidou family member I met was Sophia. Through her I met her older sister, Klea, Klea's husband, Achilles, and their daughter, Madelene. Sophia's parents, Panagiotis and Maria, became my friends as well. I was a tourist in Greece when I met them and have since returned eight times to be their houseguest.

Because of the stark differences between us, the distance in miles, and the obvious work it took to keep this friendship alive, there were numerous times I could have given up. But I can honestly say that thought never crossed my mind. I can't imagine my life without my Greek friends in it. In fact, the challenge of keeping up-to-date has been a great part of the joy.

Through the years, we have wept, laughed, mourned, and danced together. Numerous friends of mine have met Sophia when they have visited Athens. With great intensity and enthusiasm we have maintained a system of letter writing and gift giving that has bonded us even more. But the most important thing we have enjoyed together is the conversation: face-to-face, by telephone, or in those letters. We've said it all!

During my most recent visit, Klea and I had one of our usual delightful conversations. She was wearing a rather large ring I was admiring which became translucent when held up to the light. Etched into it was the Greek god, Jupiter. The exchange went something like this:

K: "Lusaki, do you know Jupiter?"
L: "You mean the Greek god, Jupiter?"
K: "Yes."
L: "Well, yes, somewhat . . . but what about him?"
K: "He is the god who changed himself into other forms to do something he wanted to do. On this ring he has changed himself into rain . . . can you see it?" (She held it up to the light.)
L: "Oh yes, I see it . . . but why did he become rain?"
K: "Because he wanted to make love with Danae."
L: "Danae? Who is Danae?"
K: (With a flick of her wrist and a thoughtful look) "Oh, I don't know . . . some Greek goddess."

I howled. Everything so serious and accurate till the end of the story; then, as though she tired of her own storytelling, "Oh, I don't know . . . some Greek goddess." I *cracked up!*

On that same trip, Klea and I had several conversations about the Lord. In fact, I walked through her door one day and the first thing she said was, "Lusaki, tell me everything you know about God." I couldn't tell her everything, but I had the opportunity to share the gospel. Little did I know that would be my last conversation with Klea. She died a few years ago of breast cancer. Across the miles, Sophia and I have tried to comfort one another in our grief. This has been a profound loss.

One of my great concerns — something I see frequently in Christian circles — is the tendency to isolate ourselves from those who are different from us. We gravitate toward people who think like we think, agree with us on everything, believe like we do, even dress the same. In so doing we miss wonderful, God-given opportunities to expand our understanding of the world and the people in it.

Jesus prayed for us about this, specifically in John 17:15 and 18: "My prayer is not that you take them out of the world but that you protect them from the evil one. . . . As you sent me into the world, I have sent them into the world."

In this world, I wouldn't have wanted to miss the Stylianidou family . . . not one single member. Don't bypass the potential for meaningful relationships just because of differences. Explore them. Embrace them. Love them.

You have left me in this world, Lord, because there are people here you love and to whom I can become your representative. Make me a loving ambassador for this divine mission. And thank you that it can be so much fun! Amen.

Twenty-Six Little Soldiers

Do nothing out of selfish ambition or vain conceit,
but in humility consider others better than yourselves.
Each of you should look not only to your own interests,
but also to the interests of others.

PHILIPPIANS 2:3–4

All my life, my favorite human invention has been the alphabet: twenty-six little soldiers ready to do battle at my command. They are all lined up there, neatly in alphabetical order, and when they are called out in squadrons, think of what they can do: They can shout orders, croon lullabies, scream in agony, whisper in ecstasy, dissolve ambiguities, resolve conflict, punctuate pretension, express tenderness, build up, or tear down. They can exaggerate or diminish. They can comfort or control. They can hurt or they can heal.

Twenty-six little letters — the alphabet! Now you tell me a *better* invention. Alone, these individual units are all but meaningless, but when they come together they can change the course of history. And that's often the way we are as people. We need each other. Two are better than one.

For example, let me turn your attention to a wonderful Old Testament passage which explains this very principle. In Ecclesiastes 4:9–12, Solomon expounds on the virtues of teamwork. He says when two work together, they have a better reward for their labor. He makes it very practical, acknowledging that when one falls the other can help him up; when two lie down they keep each other warm. He says that one can be overpowered, but two can defend themselves. This could not be more clear, and I could not agree more.

One of the reasons I like these verses is because the implication is that teamwork is not reserved for challenges of a world-changing nature, but is beneficial in the course of everyday living. For example, the idea of "two are better than one" came home to me a few years ago when a friend and I were traveling together. One day I sat down and actually made a list of why two traveling together was easier than traveling alone:

1. One can pick up coffee while the other watches the stuff.
2. One can navigate while the other drives.
3. One can take care of the other when she is sick.
4. One can do the laundry while the other makes a picnic.
5. One can exchange the money while the other retrieves the baggage.

I see this with my Women of Faith cohorts. When one of us is tired or not feeling well or burdened about something personal, the others cheer us up. We are there for each other. During the latter part of our conferences last year I had a terrible case of laryngitis, and I can't tell you the times my companions brought me water and cough drops, made me sit down in the only chair available, insisted I rest a bit longer, offered to speak in my place — all sorts of things to make my load lighter. And it was a comfort. The camaraderie and teamwork did as much to lift my spirits as did the water or chair or cough drop. How I appreciate these wonderful, unselfish women.

By reaching out to and supporting one another, we make life a lot more bearable — and more joyful as well. Marilyn, Patsy, Barbara, Sheila, Thelma, and I are accustomed to traveling alone to speaking engagements. The Women of Faith format has afforded us the opportunity to work as a team. It has been exceedingly delightful and fun. We didn't even know we needed it, but the camaraderie is unbeatable. I'd venture to say we like that part of our trips the best.

In God's economy you will be hard-pressed to find many examples of successful "Lone Rangers." Remember the power of the individual units of the alphabet coming together, and team up with somebody. Connect with a friend, a companion of your heart. You might be amazed at what you'll discover and enjoy together.

Lord, thank you for designing me for fellowship — with you, and with others. Help me be a team player so I can accomplish all you have for me to do. Refresh my soul with the love of a friend . . . and refresh her soul with my love as well. Amen.

Where's Iowa?

Whether you turn to the right or to the left, your ears will
hear a voice behind you, saying, "This is the way; walk in it."
ISAIAH 30:21

Marilyn and I were riding along in her car in the city of Riverside, California. I was navigating with a map of the area as we diligently searched for a short little street named "Iowa." The map wasn't very helpful, actually. Only the major streets were clearly delineated. Finally, after turning the map to the right and left, even upside down, I finally saw in fine print a tiny street labeled IOWA.

"Turn off on Columbia, Mar," I advised, "then make an immediate right. I'm sure it's down that way." Marilyn did exactly as I said, and after driving for several blocks, still there was no Iowa.

Marilyn made her characteristic U-turn in the middle of the street and we started back the other way. While we waited for a red light to change and pondered where on earth this little street could be, a UPS truck pulled up on our left and a beat-up old pickup truck came up on our right. The guy in the pickup yelled through our open windows to the guy in the UPS truck: "Yo, where's Iowa?"

Without the slightest hesitation, the UPS guy yelled back, "Up the street two blocks and to the left. Can't miss it." We could hardly believe it. We looked at each other while we received perfect instructions from two total strangers as they conversed through *our* car. Mar hit the gas, tootled up Columbia two blocks, and found Iowa right where it was supposed to be.

There are times when oh, what we wouldn't give for a little direction. Desperately we long for God's guidance. How many times have I heard people say, "I really want to do what God wants me to do, but what is it? What is his will anyway?" We fret and fume and sit on the sidelines waiting for a skywriter to fly by with the message, BECOME A MISSIONARY.

I've always believed that those who want to know God's will can know it. It's his responsibility to reveal it. I've never understood nor trusted people who say, "I woke up this morning and my wife was cooking bacon. I *knew* then I was supposed to go to Israel." I think God has more straightforward ways to lead his children:

1. His Word. The Bible is very definitive about the responsibility of a disciple of Christ.
2. Circumstance. God opens some doors and closes others.
3. Wise counsel. Proverbs 13:10 tells us, "Pride only breeds quarrels, but wisdom is found in those who take advice."

And consider this as a rule of thumb: God never calls without enabling us. In other words, if he calls you to do something, *he* makes it possible for you to do it. And, let me go a step further: if you don't sense his strength and ability within you to do it, I would question the call.

If God's Word, your circumstances, and the counsel of others line up, and if you sense his provision, I'd say *go for it*. And don't be surprised if, in some peculiar way, God confirms your call. Somebody in a beat-up old pickup might drive by with just the direction you need.

And if you're looking for Iowa? Give Marilyn or me a call. We know just how to get there.

I pray, Lord, that I will look for direction for my life only in you. But because you're the God of the universe, I realize you sometimes show me your way through creative, even peculiar, means. Help me to look and listen carefully to what you might be trying to tell me in some manner I never dreamed possible. May I relish the joy of knowing you are full of wonderful surprises. Amen.

God's Creative Ideas

Everything is possible for him who believes.
MARK 9:23

Tax time is usually a drag for most of us. But there are some years when, after April 15, we feel absolutely poverty-stricken. That's how I felt some years ago when my taxes were so high I had little left for the "frivolous" things of life: little luxuries like buying books, taking trips, eating out.

I put myself on a very strict budget for three months, making it a point to write down every cent I spent for even the most insignificant things, like toothpaste or a Coke. I canceled various magazines and newspapers to which I had subscriptions and thought of every way under the sun to cut costs around my house. Actually, if the truth be known, it was kinda fun.

About three weeks into this exacting self-imposed regimen I was praying one afternoon that God would give me a creative idea of how I could have a lot of fun on little money. As I was leaving the home of a friend that evening I noticed she was tossing out a mum plant simply because its blooms were wilting. I felt sorry for the plant and asked her if I could have it. Incredulously, she announced, "But it's dead." I assured her that given enough time, I could revive it. She doubted that ... which was the only challenge I needed to go full tilt boogie on a new project. *This* was the answer to my prayer. I was going to create a garden, and it wasn't going to cost me a penny.

Living in a complex where people would often toss their old dead (or dying) houseplants in the garbage bin, I began to collect everybody's discarded mum plants with no further thought. Some had been cut back, but most were just lying there with brown leaves, looking like there was no life left in them. In the course of the next three or four days I must have brought home more than twenty plants in various throes of death rattle, and began nursing them back to health.

First, I cut them all back, watered them, and placed them on the upper deck just outside my bedroom window. I sang to them and played Mozart for them. When necessary, I killed aphids with a concoction of rubbing alcohol, Murphy's Oil Soap, and water. I had become Martha Stewart. My friends accused me of making my own dirt.

I fertilized those precious little plants faithfully. In short, I *loved* them into blooming again. And *did they bloom!* I started taking pictures of them at various stages of growth: with small buds, buds just breaking into blossoms, fully blooming, and finally dying back. At one point, I'll bet I counted seven or eight hundred blooms. Magnificent hues of every color of mum in the world: yellow, orange, white, purple, rust, brown, mauve . . . they were gorgeous! And when people walked by or went outside, they looked up at that array of color. Some pointed, others took pictures, and *everybody* commented on my flower garden.

My friends who had teased me unmercifully about collecting dead plants began asking for *their* plants back. They begged me for mums. "Please, Luci, just enough for the table for my dinner party?" *No way!* Every time I looked at those sweet flowers I was reminded of God's brilliant answer to my prayer.

Have you been down in the mouth lately? Want to do something fun or uplifting for your spirit, but find yourself with no money to splurge? Ask God for a creative idea. He will give you one, and you will experience a dimension of his giving that is different from the rest. It will be restorative to your soul, because it will once again prove his ability to provide for you, even in odd, zany, off-the-wall ways.

Excuse me . . . I'd like to sit here and chat longer, but it's garbage day so I think I'll go see if I can find a few dead plants.

Father, thank you that you can create something beautiful out of what appears to be dead. You do it every day. I'm grateful for your creative ideas that cost nothing but demonstrate your love for me. Amen.

Lickety-Split!

> You will surely forget your trouble, recalling it only as waters gone by. Life will be brighter than noonday, and darkness will become like morning. You will be secure, because there is hope; you will look about you and take your rest in safety.
>
> JOB 11:16–18

Have you ever raced so fast through the day that you find yourself wondering if there really is "the sweet by-and-by" out there someplace instead of the "toils and snares" of the moment? Sometimes the concept of rest and peace seems like nothing more than a luxurious figment of the imagination.

During the thirty years I worked for Mobil Oil Corporation, hitting the freeway before dawn and dragging home after dark, I can tell you there were times I would have given anything for "the quiet life," whatever it took. I used to dream of retirement with its golf games, its manicures and pedicures, its ease and victory over the tyranny of racing to and from work. Longing for the good life, I would drive along as various cars cut in front of me, lickety-split, threatening my spiritual and mental equilibrium, not to mention the hood ornament that almost became a part of another guy's trunk.

"Lord, get me outta here!" I would scream under my breath in my most sacerdotal tone. (Look up *sacerdotal*, it's a great word!)

One morning I was in my usual snit-fit to get to work when a young man on a motorcycle raced by on my right and passed through another lane of traffic on his left. Bad move! He was going way too fast to be weaving in and out of cars that way, and everyone was giving him a piece of their mind as he zipped by. My personal loving thoughts were, *That idiot . . . he's not going to make it to the next exit if he keeps that up.*

I drove another hundred yards or so, and then the traffic really began to crawl. *Now what?* As I inched forward I began to see the metal pieces of a broken motorcycle on the shoulder of the freeway. Then I spotted the body of someone covered with a sheet. Same motorcycle. Same boy. Somewhere between where I had been and where I was now, this guy had died.

Needless to say, I was sobered and thought about little else that entire day. Even now, more than a decade later, I can still see that scene in my mind's eye. It gives me pause, partly because of the final tragedy of it all and partly because I know there are people out on that very freeway this minute, racing along just as I was . . . just as he was . . . oblivious to the fact that life is fragile. The freeway is the *last* place we think of slowing down or savoring our present moment. We simply want to get the driving over with, so we tear along with all our gripes and derring-do and madness, sometimes risking our very lives.

Even now, a number of years removed from the life I lived in the fast lane, I sometimes forget that life is fragile. The fact that I have more time to dream my dreams and take my ease is no reason at all to disregard the moment I'm in by preferring to be somewhere else. I have to remind myself that *wherever I am . . .* fast lane or slow lane, in traffic or out of traffic, racing or resting . . .

God is there. He is *in* me, abiding in me, thus making it possible for me to be all there, myself.

Every day of our lives we make choices about how we're going to live that day. Wherever we find ourselves in this fragile existence, we need to be reminded that life can be brighter than noonday and darkness like morning, because we are living fully in this moment, secure in our hope in the Lord.

Whether you're battling traffic with danger and risk on all sides, or sitting in your rocking chair knitting a sweater for your granddaughter, remember to be *all there*. Wherever you are now is God's provision, not his punishment. Celebrate *this* moment, and try very hard to do it with conscious gratitude.

Lord, I thank you for this moment — this very moment. You have given it to me to fulfill a purpose you've designed just for me. I am alive because you have something for me to do and for that, I thank you. Help me to continually realize that life is fragile. It can be snuffed out lickety-split, so don't let me race ahead or lag behind in anything. I want to live fully in the here and now. Amen.

The Secret of Fun

We proclaim to you what we have seen and heard,
so that you also may have fellowship with us.
And our fellowship is with the Father and with his Son,
Jesus Christ. We write this to make our joy complete.

1 JOHN 1:3–4

I have friends in Orlando, Florida, with whom I spend several weeks a year, including some holidays. When I visit them, we often go to one of the theme parks in the area. I can't tell you the times I have seen various families in those parks and observed this pattern: The children get tired and their whining turns to crying. This frustrates the mother, who fusses at the children. This irritates the father, who yells at the mother. I can just imagine what he's thinking: *I paid all this money and took all this time off and nobody appreciates it. When I get this bunch home, I'm never taking them anywhere again.*

As I sit on a park bench, peacefully sipping my lemonade, my heart goes out to them. Quite honestly I think everybody would be happier if they *had* stayed home.

Then I reflect on my childhood and our family vacations. We used to go to my grandfather's little bay cottage for the week or two my father had off from work. It was a modest cabin with few amenities and small rooms. Together, however, we had a wonderful time. In the mornings we fished, catching enough for a fish-fry lunch. In the afternoon we took naps, played checkers, and read; and in the evenings after dinner we told stories and jokes, put on little plays, and sang to the tune of Daddy's harmonica. In very simple ways we entertained ourselves and each other.

Since my older brother was interested in science and magic, he performed tricks and displayed his scientific wizardry while holding us in rapt attention. (He loved a captive audience.) When there was no moon, sometimes we kids were permitted to go floundering with Daddy. Boy, that was fun! He carried the Coleman lantern, swinging it back and forth as we waded about midcalf along the shoreline. When a flounder was spotted, one of us got to gig him.

I remember a couple of times when the boys went and Mother and I stayed back at the cabin. We watched from the bedroom window, singing duets as that swinging lantern disappeared out of sight. What a memory. Even now, as I write this, I can feel a full smile on my face.

Those vacations were not perfect, of course. As three very fair-skinned children, we spent half the summer burned to a crisp and the other half peeling. I'm sure there were tears and fussing and probably some irritation, but the experience of those days is incomparable in my memory.

I've often thought it is impossible to quantify a memory by the amount of planning or money spent to make it. Wonderful memories are made when the spirit is right. Therefore, it doesn't take a lot of money or an exotic setting. What it takes is an atmosphere where people can simply connect with one another. Those connections are powerful, regardless of the circumstances.

The next time you think about getting away with your loved ones, make sure you have built in times to be together. Set aside time to sing, tell stories, entertain each other . . . and laugh a lot. Create memories for yourself and your loved ones. Figure out nutty things to do that will entertain the whole family. Practice a laugh lifestyle. You can have fun anywhere.

O Lord, as I think about joy and fun, I am reminded of 1 Timothy 6:17 that instructs us not to trust in the uncertainty of wealth but to put our hope in God, who richly provides us with everything for our enjoyment. Thank you for the laughter you create in the fellowship of being together with those we love. It is a gift of your grace. Amen.

Be Your Own Source of Comedy

We rejoice in the hope of the glory of God.
ROMANS 5:2

Several years ago I put a sum of money in Fidelity Federal Bank and locked it into a certificate of deposit. Five years later it came to maturity, and I had to make a decision whether to lock it in again or take the money out. With my financial advisor's advice I determined that it was time to take it out, and I set the wheels in motion to do that through the mail.

In conjunction with this CD I had also opened a little checking account in Fidelity Federal in the amount of $500, with the assurance that if that minimum amount was kept in the account at all times, I would receive a quarter of a percent interest which would also go into the CD account. Not a big sum, but worth having nonetheless.

Once I determined to reinvest the CD proceeds elsewhere, this freed me, I reasoned, to take out the $500 as well. I was thrilled. Here I would have $500 that I'd sort of forgotten about (since I couldn't touch it anyway) to play with. "Christmas is coming," I thought. "This is great timing!"

About three days before the CD transaction was to be made I received in the mail a statement from my checking account, advising that an interest charge of $11.88 had been levied against that account, which not only brought the sum below the $500 I had carefully left untouched, but had come to me out of the blue. I simply couldn't understand why on earth I would get such a statement. *Why, I haven't even used this account,* I muttered to myself. *I've never even written a check. What does this mean anyway? I hate this.*

Well, I thought, *I'll just go to Fidelity Federal and set things straight.*

The next day on my way to speak at a university, I passed a branch office of the bank. *I'll stop there on the way home and clear this up,* I said to myself as I drove by. Which is exactly what I did. I parked in front of the bank, grabbed the statement, flounced inside, marched right up to the teller, and pontificated, "You know, I don't understand this. Here I get this statement in the mail informing me of a charge of $11.88, but I've never even used this account. I mean, this is crazy. I'd like you to waive this service charge, please, and give me a check for $500 right now. Can you do that immediately?"

The whole time the woman behind the counter had said nothing, just looked at the paper, then at me. When I finished blasting out my request she finally said, "Well, I'd like to, lady, but this is Wells Fargo and your account is at Fidelity Federal."

The village idiot, crawling out the bank's side door, heard the tellers whispering among themselves: "Can you believe that woman came in here demanding money, and she doesn't even have an account in this bank? Can ya beat that?"

I got in my car and laughed my head off. What else could I do but enjoy my own mistake?

We've *got* to be able to laugh at our own mistakes. At least I do — I'm so experienced at making them.

Don't take yourself too seriously. It just makes life all the harder. It'll all come out in the wash anyway, because God's glory eventually will eclipse everything that goes wrong on this earth.

Lighten up and learn to laugh at yourself. None of us is infallible. We make mistakes in life, and more often than not, they're funny. Sometimes, being your own source of comedy is the most fun of all.

Jesus, help me to see the humor in everyday occurrences. And when I make mistakes, remind me it isn't the end of the world. It's a learning experience, an opportunity to laugh and to trust your sovereignty. Amen.

Joy, Joy, Joy . . . Forevermore Without Conditions

> Now when a man works, his wages are not credited to him
> as a gift, but as an obligation. However, to the man who
> does not work but trusts God who justifies the wicked, his
> faith is credited as righteousness.
>
> ROMANS 4:4–5

Here's what I hate: you open up your mailbox, and crammed in with the mail you want to receive is a huge envelope with your name in big letters on the front. *LUCI SWINDOLL, YOU HAVE JUST WON ONE MILLION DOLLARS, CONGRATULATIONS!!!* Inside the envelope is the postscript in little tiny letters: *if your number is called.* Oh, boy! And your immediate thought is, *you can't get something for nothing.*

Or how 'bout this: you open your mail and staring you in the face is an opportunity to fly free. *Oh, wow . . . free!* Then you read on: " . . . if you will just open a credit card account with American Express." Well, okay. So you open the account. Your free ticket comes in the mail, and on it you read: *Certain conditions apply . . . please see other side.* And the conditions? Well, in order to use this particular ticket which is nonnegotiable, nontransferable, and non-refundable, you must fly on a Tuesday night only between the hours of 11 P.M. and 2 A.M. sitting only in a middle seat with no carry-on luggage on a flight going east only with four stops on the way to Paducah, Kentucky. And your immediate thought is, *you can't get something for nothing*.

Or, here's a good one: you find a flyer under your windshield wiper—one night in a resort hotel is yours . . . absolutely free. No cost. No obligation. No restriction. However . . . the free night must follow ten consecutive nights in that same room in that same hotel. And your immediate thought is—you got it, *you can't get something for nothing.*

Then, you pick up your New Testament and turn to Ephesians 2:8–9, and there in bold print you read these comforting words: "For it is by grace you have been saved, through faith—and this not from yourselves, it is the gift of God—not by works, so that no one can boast."

The wonderful thing about the Christian life is that we all enter freely. No matter who you are, where you're from, what your experience has been, Jesus Christ invites you to freely come. No conditions. No restrictions. No small print. No waiting. About this, you can be certain.

My favorite theological doctrine is "justification." It is the sovereign act of God whereby he declares the believing sinner righteous, while still in a sinning state. In other words, when a person comes to God, just as she is— while still in her sinning state—God looks at her and, because of what Jesus Christ did on the cross, he proclaims her righteous. She does not have to clean up her act. She does not have to do penance. She does not have to be thin or good-looking or rich or famous or accomplished. All she has to do is believe God for the forgiveness of her sins.

If you have never made the wonderful discovery of knowing Christ personally, you can do so at this very moment. Know that God loves you unconditionally; know that Christ died on the cross to pay the penalty for your sins; know that upon your invitation he will come into your life, forgive your sins, and begin a personal relationship with you. There is no waiting. Once you place your faith in him, you can be sure that you have eternal life. In fact, he is preparing a place for your comfort, every consecutive night for all eternity.

Salvation is a gift. He gives. You receive. Pray a simple prayer like this:

Lord Jesus, I need you. I want to know you personally. Thank you for dying on the cross for my sins. I open the door of my life and receive you as my Savior and Lord. Thank you for forgiving me and giving me eternal life. Take control of my life and make me the kind of person you want me to be. Amen.

Dwayne's Day

One man considers one day more sacred than another;
another man considers every day alike.
Each one should be fully convinced in his own mind.
He who regards one day as special, does so to the Lord.
ROMANS 14:5–6

An edict went out from the board to offer an additional holiday to all Mobil employees. This was like a breath of fresh air around the laboratory where I worked. We were thrilled. Forms were sent out for everyone to submit his or her day of preference.

My friend Doris, a secretary, asked her boss his request. Dwayne was a rather unconventional but highly intelligent Ph.D.

"August 12," Dwayne said.

"August 12? Are you sure?"

"Well . . . yeah. Why do you ask? Have a lot of people requested that day?"

"No. No one. I guess I wonder why you do."

"Because it's a Friday. I like Fridays off."

"But next year it won't be Friday."

"Oh, that's right. . . . Well, what have most people requested?"

"Most people want the day after Thanksgiving."

"But I already take that Friday as a day of vacation."

A bit exasperated, Doris tried to calmly state the obvious. "Dwayne, if the company gives you the day off, you wouldn't *have* to take it as a vacation day. It would already *be* a holiday. You'd have a long weekend . . . you know, four days together."

With all the seriousness in the world, Dwayne shot back, "Then what day would I take as a day of vacation?"

Giving up, Doris replied, "How 'bout August 12?"

That settled it for Dwayne. "Great idea."

Doris shook her head and walked away.

I've laughed at this story for years. Dear, sweet Dwayne, brilliant but baffled by such simple things. Every August 12 I think of him. I do something different that day . . . phone one of my old pals from the laboratory in Dallas and chat . . . bake a batch of muffins in Dwayne's honor . . . look through photos from the sixties, and remember my friends from the Mobil lab.

I like having special days set aside to commemorate an event: birthdays, anniversaries, graduations. My journals are full of remembrances like "Forty years ago today my parents were married." Or "Six years ago I broke my leg." Or "If my father had lived, he'd be ninety today." Or "Remember, Luci, three years ago you bought this house."

Days are important. I anticipate them. I'm looking forward to the day my friends come for Thanksgiving, to the next time I'll see my brother in Florida. And I can never quite wait for Christmas.

The word *days* appears more than five hundred times in Scripture, and the Mosaic Law prescribed feast days when the congregation was to celebrate by dancing, singing, resting from labor, and giving praise to God. These were occasions of joy and gladness.

I encourage you to create special days for yourself and your family. Twenty-four hours when you do something entirely different from other days . . . or maybe do nothing. Barbara Johnson declares the first day of each month a holiday. She reserves it just *for herself.* She calls me and says, "Take a bath and change your sheets. It's the first day of the month!" These twelve days are singular and individual to Barbara. I love that!

The happiest people I know are those who are fully convinced in their own minds that *this* is the day the Lord has made. They rejoice and are glad in it. Celebrate *all* your days—including August 12.

Give us joy this day, Lord, in knowing you. And help us remember that every day we are alive is your gift to us. Amen.

Monday Musings

Whatever you do, work at it with all your heart,
as working for the Lord, not for men, since you know
that you will receive an inheritance from the Lord as a
reward. It is the Lord Christ you are serving.
COLOSSIANS 3:23–24

Mondays . . . too many chores. Since I travel most weekends, Monday is the day I unpack. That's always a mess, with stuff strewn everywhere and suitcases lying about. Being a neat-nick, I hate that.

Then there's the laundry . . . piles of clothes that need washing. And those piles multiply in the night! I have this theory that, after the Lord comes and time is no more, somewhere, in a corner of the world, dirty laundry will still be waiting, multiplying.

On Monday I must make stops at the grocery store, the cleaners, the bank, the post office, the service station, the hairdresser . . . Deliver me! Mondays annoy me.

But . . . not completely. In another way, I love Mondays. I love unloading all my stuff out of the suitcase and organizing it back where it belongs. That satisfies me. I love pulling fresh laundry from the dryer and folding it while it's still warm.

And, frankly, I've grown to love the bank. Why, I have my own teller. Her name is Gwen. She's a sweetheart with a ready smile and a warm heart. She's a Christian who's helpful and patient. I give her books my brother and Women of Faith have written. She loves that, and I experience such joy in making her happy. We have great chats.

And, you know, I also love grocery shopping. I love having all those choices and anticipating the preparation of wonderful meals. I grab up fresh bouquets of flowers and never quite seem to get the smile off my face. Every now and then, I add a jar of pickles, can of hair spray, or package of liverwurst to another shopper's unattended cart, just to entertain myself and give that person whiplash at the checkout counter.

Even the post office can be rewarding. I love buying stamps. Last week, I bought ten stamps and gave two each to the five people behind me. I told them I hated waiting in line and was sure they did too. But, for doing so, I was giving them a little present. My own little random act of kindness.

On Monday nights, I feel genuine joy, having such a sense of accomplishment. Plus, I've had a few good laughs, enjoyed a meaningful chat or two, and expressed love in a tangible way to total strangers.

So what's the difference? Why do I sometimes get bogged down with chores, hating the day? Then, at other times, I get fired up with enthusiasm, loving the day? Perspective! Perspective is everything. Paul encourages us to do whatever we do with all our hearts. He tells us to put our soul into it. Like the old song says, "You gotta have heart." When you do, you can do anything. The busiest days can become our most joyful.

We all have things in life we have to do, but we can choose how we want to do them. It's up to each of us. I can tell you this, though. There's only one way to have joy . . . by doing everything "as unto the Lord."

By the way, if you're the one who arrived at home with an extra jar of pickles, enjoy them. Toss them in a salad and look at it this way: You helped bring a smile to someone today. Perspective is everything.

Help us realize, Father, that life is what we make it. Teach us to make it new every morning . . . fun, fresh, and fulfilling. We thank you that you care about every day of our lives — even Mondays! Amen.

The Eyes of the Heart

The LORD does not look at the things man looks at.
Man looks at the outward appearance,
but the LORD looks at the heart.
1 SAMUEL 16:7

The filthy station wagon pulled into the car wash, loaded with kids and a driver who looked as if he hadn't shaved in weeks. With his hair tousled and a cigarette hanging out of the right side of his mouth, he was wearing clothes he probably had slept in. When he stopped, all eyes turned toward him.

Hairy Dicer, if I ever saw one, I thought to myself. A friend of mine called anybody "Hairy Dicer" who had those little fur dice hanging from the rearview mirror. This guy took the prize.

He opened the back of the wagon and began to lift out the occupants. One by one he hugged and kissed each child, whom he gently lowered to the ground. Then they romped and played with one another and their father to their little hearts' content. I knew they were his children because over and over they called him "Daddy."

"Oh, Daddy, play with us. Daddy, throw me the ball. Look, Daddy, look at this. I can do that, Daddy . . . watch!"

Slowly, lovingly, deliberately, this disheveled man gave attention to all six children, playing, talking, laughing, discovering . . . and together they had a wonderful time. I sat, astonished and ashamed of myself for thinking the guy was a creep.

How quickly we judge another's outward appearance. It's so easy to do, isn't it? We see clothes that don't match, and we judge. We don't like a person's hair so we judge. We look at another's car, manners, music, posture, or facial characteristics . . . judging all the while.

I'll tell you, if the human perspective had been the criterion for God's judgment, the Swindolls would have been zapped long ago. Each of us, my brothers and I, live the majority of our lives in well-worn clothes that don't match. Comfortable is what we like. More often than not, I go to the store in my oldest sweats. They're perfect. They fit the contours of my aging body and feel great. I don't want to change clothes just to pick up a carton of milk, grab a hamburger, or have the car washed. My friends encourage me to wear designer sweats. Not on your life!

In his book, *The Little Prince,* Antoine de Saint-Exupéry states the principle, "It is only with the heart that one can see rightly; what is essential is invisible to the eye."

Oh, how I love that thought. "What is essential is invisible" captures what we read in Scripture. Not only do we have no right to pass judgment on another, but we also have no way to see what's inside that person.

Who cares if the guy at the car wash was the opposite of my view of a proper dad? All those kids cared about was the attention he gave them. He listened. He played. He loved them.

And, you know what is really amazing? When I saw his heart . . . with my heart . . . he became almost good-looking. Well, maybe not good-looking, but certainly more appealing. I saw him with different eyes, the eyes of nonjudgment. I liked him.

When I don't put any judgmental demands on others, I'm happiest because I know I'm doing what is right. I feel good. When nobody puts demands on me, it frees me to be who I really am — a slob, clothed in Christ's righteousness.

Oh, Father, help us be obedient to your Word, which says to accept one another as you, in Christ Jesus, have accepted us. Amen.

Five-Finger Exercise

Whoever can be trusted with very little can also be trusted with much, and whoever is dishonest with very little will also be dishonest with much. So if you have not been trustworthy in handling worldly wealth, who will trust you with true riches?

LUKE 16:10–11

I'd studied the models in the hobby shop window for days. Three balsa airplanes. Seven bucks. Where was I going to get the money? My allowance wasn't quite enough. Finally, borrowing from one of my brothers, I ran to the store, bought the models, and hurried home to show my parents. I spread everything out on the table and explained how I was going to carve, build, and paint these cute little airplanes. I couldn't wait to start.

"Just a minute," Mother said. "How much did they cost?"

"Seven dollars and fifty cents. I saved the seven and borrowed fifty cents from Babe."

Then my father joined the discussion. "Did you spend all the money you had on models?"

"Yes, sir."

Calmly, but with a serious expression, Daddy said, "Honey, buying models isn't a bad thing. They're fun to make, and I'm sure you'll enjoy them. But spending everything you have on one purchase is not wise. Some-day, when you're grown, you are going to be responsible for your own money. If you use it carefully, you'll always have some."

Then he opened his hand, and pointing to each finger as he stated each principle, he said, "Spend some, save some, tithe some, invest some, and give some away. If you do this, you'll never have to worry about money."

That was my first course in stewardship. I was ten. And now, I remember his lesson. When applied, I can tell you it works.

Money is a medium of exchange. It's the tool with which we barter. It enables us to do things. To own things. To enjoy things. It is not an end in itself; it's a means to an end. When we keep that straight, we'll resolve much of the angst we experience regarding money.

God instructs us to be good stewards, and when we obey this instruction, money is not a problem. Read Luke 16:10–11 again. It says if you're a good steward of little, you can be trusted with more. Even much.

I follow simple but practical principles about handling money. These guidelines help me make wise financial choices. They help me control my money without it controlling me.

1. Tithe off my gross income.
2. Live within my means.
3. Take care of what I have.
4. Wear it out.
5. Do it myself.
6. Anticipate my needs.
7. Consider multiple use.
8. Make gifts.
9. Shop less.
10. Buy used.
11. Pay cash.
12. Do without.

Let me give you three other suggestions that I find helpful: First, if the pleasure of having something is sweeter to you than the pain of paying it off, don't be afraid of indebtedness. But you must manage it.

Second, if you see others affording things you can't, stop comparing. Scripture says when we compare ourselves, we are not wise.

Third, if you want to be the happiest person in town, give away more than you keep. It is indeed more blessed (joyful) to give than to receive.

As a daughter of the King, remember this: No matter how little money is in your purse, you're already rich anyway. You may be broke, but you'll never be poor.

Loving Father, give me what it takes to take care of what you give me. And help me to remember everything I have is yours. Amen.

Up, Up, and Away

For nothing is impossible with God.
LUKE 1:37

It was one of the most exciting things I've ever done. You should see my pictures. There we were, one hundred invited guests gathered in a private area to watch the liftoff of Atlantis. At 10:37 P.M., in clear, balmy Florida, the shuttle soared heavenward. Fire, steam, smoke, clicking cameras, yelling, whistling, shouting . . . and then KA-BOOM! Off they went. I loved that moment. It took my breath away, and I was so proud to be an American.

I was a guest of astronaut Wendy Lawrence, who left Earth for a ten-day mission. Wendy is a woman of strong personal faith in Christ, and I delighted in praying for her and the others before they left. During those days the Atlantis spent in orbit, I was immensely more interested in the space program than ever before. I even went outside every night and looked up just in case I could wave to Wendy. And I prayed for them until they were safely home.

The instant that shuttle lifted off and was so quickly beyond Earth's bonds, I was mesmerized. Talk about defying odds, breaking barriers, not being held back . . . what a graphic illustration! Even the force of gravity did not hold back that little ship.

I know people like that. And, if you'll pardon the pun, I gravitate toward them. They're a source of encouragement to me. They hang tough when others give up, forge ahead when others lag behind, choose to be cheerful when others sink in defeat. People like my friend Charlotte.

Char defies the odds. After multiple surgeries and chronic health problems, she maintains the most incredible attitude. Every time I chat with her on the phone, she is reticent to talk about herself because she's so busy asking about me: "Now where are you? Oh, I've been there, and I love it too. You say it's snowing? Golly, I remember when I was there, and . . ." Off and running. No self-pity, no martyrdom, no self-centeredness. Her spirit soars, though her body fails. When I hang up, I feel better.

One of the pioneers of Starbucks Coffee Company writes in his book, *Pour Your Heart Into It,* "Once you overcome seemingly insurmountable obstacles, other hurdles become less daunting. Most people can achieve beyond their dreams if they insist upon it. I'd encourage everyone to dream big, lay your foundations well, absorb information like a sponge, and not be afraid to defy conventional wisdom. Just because it hasn't been done before doesn't mean you shouldn't try it."*

I feel the strength of those words as they lift off the page. Yet even more powerful are the words of Jesus, who challenged his followers to move mountains, walk on water, and prepare a picnic for five thousand. He assured us we would do no less than the impossible.

I don't know the circumstances of your life. Maybe, like my friend Charlotte, you have health problems. Maybe you're experiencing a financial crisis, a relational struggle, or a genuine feeling of inadequacy. Whatever

---

*Howard Schultz, *Pour Your Heart Into It* (New York: Hyperion, 1997), 19.

your biggest problems, be sure you aren't surrendering to the odds. You may look at yourself and say, "I can't. I can't rise above this, get beyond it, or overcome it," and so you give up. Don't quit, my friend. You're just starting this ride. You have the whole sky above your head. God wants to free you from bondage, and he knows just how to do it.

Father, you don't always do exactly what I think you will, but you can do the impossible. Lift my spirits and help me soar. Amen.

Mere Inconvenience or Major Catastrophe?

The fear of the LORD leads to life:
Then one rests content, untouched by trouble.
PROVERBS 19:23

I found an article in the *London Times* that tells about a farmer's woeful day. Badly crushed under his tractor and temporarily blinded, he staggered home three-quarters of a mile, then took off his boots to avoid dirtying the kitchen floor.

Fred Williamson had been using the headlights of the tractor for illumination while he repaired a water tank in the field. The hand brake failed, and the tractor ran over him, ripping his face with barbed wire caught in the tractor's wheels. Mr. Williamson suffered broken ribs and collarbone, a punctured lung, and damage to his face that rendered him unrecognizable.

After the accident, he managed to turn off the tractor and close the gates behind him. He walked home and said to his wife, "Don't panic, Mary, but I need an ambulance." His jaw and cheekbones were broken, and his nose was in a thousand pieces. His left eye was missing. His wife said the first thing he asked her after his eight hours of surgery was if the water tank had been fixed.

Now, I have to admire that man. Of all people with a right to complain, Fred Williamson is one. However, I also have to laugh because Mr. Williamson took my philosophical approach to life to its extreme.

You see, when I hear people complaining, I often think, *They can't distinguish between a mere inconvenience and a major catastrophe.* We need to recognize the vast difference between the two. Nobody ever said life is easy, trouble free, or without problems. Everyone knows that. The secret to handling problems is how we view them. It's an attitude thing. Running out of coffee is inconvenient. A rained-out picnic is inconvenient. But a smashed jaw, broken cheekbone, crushed nose, and missing eye? We're talking catastrophe!

This past summer while traveling with a friend in the British Isles, we had a flat tire on our little rented car. Bummer! On a curve, a huge bus had taken its half of the road out of the middle, forcing us to run into a rock fence, flattening the tire, ruining the hubcap, and denting the fender. We managed to wobble the car down the road to a farmhouse, where we used the phone and waited for the repairman.

To some people this would have been a major catastrophe. After all, it wasn't our car, we were in a foreign country, we had no idea how much the repair would cost, and it took precious time out of our day. But that wasn't our feeling. While sitting on a rock waiting, we had a spectacular view of Ireland's coastline and plenty of laughter. Neither of us will ever forget the incident, and photos captured the memory.

Maybe I'm just a cockeyed optimist, but I think life is to be experienced joyfully rather than endured grudgingly. We know it brings complexities and trouble. Scripture affirms that. But why do we take minor irritations so seriously? Why do we act as though it's the end of the world? Think of the pain and conflict we would spare ourselves, the stress we would forego, if we just realized mere inconveniences can be survived.

This is all part of "resting content, untouched by trouble," as the verse for today describes it. It's believing when you trust God, regardless of the circumstances, you have "life, happiness, and protection from harm" (Prov. 19:23 TLB).

The next time something gets you down and you want to whine or complain, remember Fred Williamson.

Father, give us the grace to rest content in you no matter what. Teach us to trust. Amen.

Flirting with Danger

Charm is deceptive, and beauty is fleeting;
but a woman who fears the LORD is to be praised.
PROVERBS 31:30

My favorite place to travel is Africa. The place is filled with intrigue, risk, and adventure, but when one is on safari, the continent is even more fascinating.

The highlight of any safari is seeing a leopard. Most people never do. I know folks who have lived in East Africa for years but who have never seen this elusive animal. Nocturnal, solitary, and enormously independent, the leopard is also secretive and sensually seductive. Prowling the savanna by night, it silently stalks its prey, makes the kill, and hauls it into the limbs of a tree. All of which means the leopard is athletic and intelligent. An incomparable beast of breathtaking beauty!

My friend Mary and I had been on a photographic safari for a week. We had not just seen but had studied the animals in their own environment. I had forty rolls of exposed film in my bag, and our journals were chock-full of the splendor of our adventure. It had been perfect except for one thing: no leopard. Everyone told us that few were lucky enough to see the leopard. We shouldn't count on it.

Then, on the last day of our safari, as we were about to say good night to the African bush, we saw a gorgeous leopard strolling toward us with all the arrogance in the world. Our driver stopped. So did the leopard. He turned and sat upright next to us. He was posing. The setting added to the magnificence of the moment. It was like a George Innes painting. The dirt in that part of Kenya is a deep rust and rich with nutrients. The foliage was every shade of green, and the sky was comprised of gray, blue, and indigo. With this as his backdrop, the leopard sat in his slinky, spotted fur coat. His cold, intense, unblinking stare gave us goose bumps as we made eye contact with the beast.

After snapping three rolls of film, we reluctantly drove away. Almost immediately the driver stopped the truck and whispered casually, "Oh, theh is anotheh le-o-pard. You are veddy lucky with this miracle."

It wasn't luck at all. We had prayed to see a leopard. As we watched our second one in the same day, I relaxed and felt bold. He was so . . . close. So comfortable in our presence. So . . . charming. I wanted to reach out and pet him. I considered him a friend. I knew he was wild, but in that instant, he seemed tame.

How many times have you been in a similar situation? Something seems so innocent, so safe. You don't realize that what feels right has the potential to destroy. Scripture points this out in Proverbs 16:25, "There is a way that seems right to a man, but in the end it leads to death." It could be death of a relationship, finances, health, or life itself.

Predators are real. That's not a problem as long as we keep our distance. But when we drop our guard and feel comfortable, we are lured, then hooked, then devoured. We wonder how something so beautiful and charming could have been the messenger of death.

God's way of escape for his followers is to keep our eyes on the Lord, to fear and reverence him. Don't be enticed by a perfect setting, colorful surroundings, or beautiful creatures. The seductive predator might be lying in wait, ready to have you for lunch.

Our loving, overseeing Father, keep us focused on you so we are not drawn away by that which breaks our hearts and our lives. Amen.

Who Am I?

God said to Moses, "I AM WHO I AM."
EXODUS 3:14

But by the grace of God I am what I am.
1 CORINTHIANS 15:10

I've never had an identity crisis. Nonetheless, I'm constantly clarifying who I am. The conversation goes like this:

"I love your husband. I listen to him on *Insight for Living*."

"He's my brother."

"Aren't you his wife?"

"No, I'm his sister."

And then, with obvious disappointment and disillusionment, "But I thought you were his wife."

"No."

"Then the two of you aren't married?"

Finally, feeling sympathetic, I apologize. "I'm sorry. I'm not married to him."

With utter frustration, "But, why not? I told my friends you were his wife."

Please! I've often thought of wearing a sign, "No, I'm not his wife." I love the guy dearly, but I'm not married to him.

Not only do I experience this bit of confusion over my relationship to my brother, but there's also this voice of mine. It's always been low. My brothers used to tease me about being my own grandfather. As a voice major in college, I was contralto. In choirs, I choose the lowest harmonic note. But here's the most fun: in the wee morning hours, when I order breakfast in hotel rooms, they respond, "Yes, sir. Right away, sir." I play a little game with the phone. I look it squarely in the dial and say aloud, "It isn't 'sir.'" Even in Scotland, the operator said, "Aye . . . and we'll 'ave it right up to ya, laddie." It isn't "laddie."

I'm not "laddie," not "sir," not my own grandfather, and definitely not Chuck's wife. So who am I? Me. I'm myself. No other. No duplicate. No clone. Luci Swindoll — me.

Psalm 100:3 says, "Know that the LORD is God. It is he who made us, and we are his; we are his people, the sheep of his pasture." That pretty much settles it for me. Always has. He created me, and I'm who he wants me to be. Nothing more. Nothing less. Nothing else. That's true for you, as well.

The poet e. e. cummings wrote:

To be nobody but yourself in a world which is doing its best, night and day, to make you everybody else — means to fight the hardest battle which any human being can fight; and never stop fighting.

I keep that in my address book as a reminder to be who I am, whom God made me.

The writer of Job says each of us has been uniquely shaped by God's hand. He has formed us exactly. The great I AM made us and shaped us. A blessed thought! I don't have to be anybody but me. And, as I walk with Christ, he's in the process of making me more like himself. God created us who we are and "nothing is to be rejected" (1 Tim. 4:4).

Being who you are is sometimes difficult because you don't like who you are. Accept yourself as God's wonderful creation. Then you are free to be you without fear. I love hearing Sheila Walsh say again and again, "When someone asks me who I am, I say, 'I'm Sheila Walsh, the daughter of the King.'" Go, Sheila!

I've heard Chuck say repeatedly: "Sis, know yourself, be yourself, like yourself." Wise words.

Who are you? God's unique creation. There's nobody just like you. Never has been, never will be. Only you can be you. Be whom God made you.

Father, we want to be comfortable with who we are. Work in us that we might be all you created us to be. Forgive us for rejecting your creation. Amen.

Two Are Better Than One

Two are better than one, because they have a good return
for their work: If one falls down, his friend can help him up.
ECCLESIASTES 4:9–10

Sometimes I think I'm the Lone Ranger. I'm the picture of solitude and independence. I entertain myself for days with no help from anyone.

But that isn't always the case. Every now and then I feel the need for connectedness. I want to be surrounded by my circle of friends. Being alone just doesn't cut it. That's what happened one summer when I started out thinking I was the Lone Ranger.

I was in Ireland with a friend. On the day we were scheduled to fly to Scotland, I awakened feeling ill, chilled, and nauseated. My friend suggested we reschedule our flight, but I insisted I'd be fine. I fully intended to rise up and walk, to get myself packed, dressed, to the airport, and on to the next country on our itinerary. I was sure I wouldn't need any help, being the Lone Ranger and all. . . . In the meantime, I went back to bed.

When I awakened from my feverish stupor, my traveling companion had gathered up my things, packed my bags, and made all the arrangements for us to leave. She asked again if I wanted to delay our departure. Of course not! I insisted I'd be fine. The minute we climbed in the cab, I fell sound asleep.

Arriving at the airport, again I heard, "Do you want to leave later?" Of course not! I insisted I'd be fine. So while I rested in a wheelchair inside the terminal, she stood in line, checked in our bags, and collected our boarding passes. I fell fast asleep in the chair.

This went on all day, with my insisting I could make it on my own while she did both my part and hers. I fell asleep every time I found a place to sit.

Ultimately, we arrived at the hotel in Scotland. While she made sure our possessions were brought to the room, found a drugstore, and bought medicine, I crawled into bed.

It wasn't until the next day I figured out how I got there. I had had a caretaker in my time of need . . . one who joyfully provided for me when I was oblivious to her acts of kindness and hard work.

That's the way life is, isn't it? We need each other. Scripture says two are better than one. We're instructed to love, pray for, care about, accept, forgive, serve, encourage, and build up one another.

I love that about my partners in the Women of Faith conferences. We bebop all over the country watching out for each other. We serve one another joyfully, from the heart. When one of us is down, we rally to her. When one celebrates, we rejoice together. We're a team. We never anticipated this kind of bonding, but bonded we are.

People need each other — no matter how much we insist we don't. Nobody is an island, an entity unto herself, or a Lone Ranger. We're in this thing called *community,* and part of the joy of community is sharing the weight. The weight of burdens, losses, loneliness, and fear.

Look around you, my friend. Who's there for you? And who are you there for? Take a careful look. Even those who insist they can make it on their own may just be waiting for you to reach out and help. Be there and available. Even the Lone Ranger had a sidekick.

Father, thank you we are not alone. You are with us. Always. And you give us the gift of friendship. Don't let us miss the joy of it. Amen.

Keep Patching

Now we ask you, brothers, to respect those
who work hard among you, who are over you in the Lord
and who admonish you. Hold them in the highest regard
in love because of their work.

1 THESSALONIANS 5:12–13

A number of years ago I read an article in the *Los Angeles Times* that I kept. It's about a graduate of Whitworth College who anonymously provided seventeen faculty members with vacations, gifts, and various gestures of kindness to say thanks for an education that changed his life. One teacher, on returning from a trip to Hawaii, said, "I look for ways now to express my own generosity." The whole idea had a ricochet effect.

In the book *Tuesdays with Morrie,* written as a tribute to a teacher, the author tells of the life-changing lessons he learned from his old Brandeis University prof, Morrie Schwartz, who was on his deathbed. Every Tuesday for fourteen weeks the former student, Mitch Albom, went to Morrie's home, where they discussed the world, family, emotions, money, the fear of aging, and forgiveness. Each Tuesday Mitch learned words of wisdom, encouragement, and love, imparted by an old man to his young friend.

It reminded me of my favorite college professor, Florence Bergendahl, or Bergie, as we called her. What a character! She was tall, with a majestic presence, perfect posture, a purposeful stride, and booming voice. She barked out pet phrases and short homilies: "Straighten up . . . never slouch . . . a good soloist stands tall and gets down to business. Remember your voice is *you,* so speak up . . . sing up . . . let us hear *you* behind that sound box."

On Saturday afternoons Bergie turned up the Metropolitan Opera broadcast full blast as she putted golf balls down the hallway of the teacher's dorm. When that little ball entered the tilted cup at the far end, she would gleefully laugh and, with full voice, sing along with the radio.

I studied voice with Bergie, but from her I learned some of life's greatest lessons. We discussed music, art, travel, lifestyles, books, learning, loving, and losing. She once said to me, "Life is like a patchwork quilt with joys and sorrows, gains and losses, fullness and hunger, and until you die, you'll keep patching. This is what gives meaning to life."

I loved her dearly, and when I sing, I think of her and her profound investment in my life. With every note that comes from my mouth, I am thankful for what she gave me.

Sometimes I wonder if we've lost the art of expressing gratitude. We miss the joy of verbalizing appreciation, and we rob others of the joy of hearing how grateful we are. We don't know what to say or do.

As today's Scripture points out, we should respect those who have worked hard among us. Give back—not necessarily a plane ticket to a foreign country or a published manuscript, but something to reflect the value of the investment made . . . and something from the heart. That's how the giving continues. Someone gives to us . . . we give to another . . . they, to another . . . and on it goes. As Barbara Johnson says, it's boomerang joy bursting out all over.

Mitch Albom ends his tribute to Morrie with these questions: "Have you ever really had a teacher? One who saw you as a raw but precious thing, a jewel that, with wisdom, could be polished to a proud shine?"*

Does someone come to mind? Ask the Lord to give you a creative way to thank that person for his or her gift to you. "Hold them in the highest regard in love because of their work."

Lord Jesus, our greatest teacher, instruct us how to express our appreciation to those who have labored hard, helping us to grow. Amen.

---

*Mitch Albom, *Tuesdays with Morrie* (New York: Doubleday, 1997), 192.

Alive Again

Every good and perfect gift is from above,
coming down from the Father of the heavenly lights,
who does not change like shifting shadows.

JAMES 1:17

This joy that I have, the world didn't give it to me,
This joy that I have, the world didn't give it to me.
The world didn't give it . . .
And the world can't take it away.

Oh, my sisters, listen up! I've been singing that song for days, as I'm running around the house, in the street, at the grocery store, in restaurants. Everywhere. "This Joy That I Have" has become my song. Actually, Thelma gave me the song, but God gave me the joy.

Here's what happened: For fifteen years I've had sleep apnea, which is a disorder that causes one to hold one's breath during the night for long periods of time. More often than not, the person awakens repeatedly in an effort to breathe. Very little sleep results. There is never REM sleep, the deepest and most necessary of all.

In an overnight stay at a sleep clinic, I learned that in 102 minutes of so-called "sleep," I awakened myself 123 times, with 87 of those being apnea episodes, where I gasped for breath. I'm surprised I didn't die somewhere along the way.

But, instead of dying, I slept during most of my "waking" hours. I slept while talking on the phone or face-to-face. I slept while writing, reading, driving. I slept at the computer, standing in line, or sitting in a chair. I slept at meetings, while eating, in moving vehicles, or while they were parked. I fell asleep mid-sentence. I slept at parties or in the quietness of my own home, at my desk, or standing at the stove. I slept all the time, and I drove my loved ones to distraction.

They begged me to get help, but I put it off. I kept thinking I would get better, the condition would go away, or Jesus would come.

Now we know I never really slept, night or day. I just dozed. I even dozed on the "porch" while waiting to speak. My greatest fear was I'd fall asleep during my own message. I didn't, and we all considered it a miracle.

Then I got brave. I phoned a specialist and found the cure. It's called a CPAP unit. It's a heaven-sent contraption that fits like a mask over my nose, permitting me to breathe deeply for the first time in almost two decades. I actually sleep! The air comes only through a hose connected to a calibrated motor so there's no sound from the mouth. I can't yawn, talk, snore, or draw in air while wearing the mask. I can do only one thing . . . sleep. It's wonderful.

So what if I'm funny looking? So what if I sleep with a tube of air attached? So what if I just increased my carry-on luggage by another bag? I don't care because I'm sleeping, girls. It's fabulous!

If you've put off something you know needs attention, put it off no longer. Get up now and make the phone call that will change your life. Reach out and take the gift God wants to give you. Stop procrastinating. His gifts are good and perfect.

I'm a new woman. I'm alive again, singing, dancing, and bouncing off the ceiling. I'm wearing my friends out. Oh, well, I may have to get a new set of friends, anyway. Ones with more energy.

"This joy that I have, the world . . ."

Father, thank you that your gifts are good and perfect. Thank you for your provision for us. Prompt us to be responsible and attentive when we need to do something, and help us do it now. Amen.

I Remember It Well

Remember the wonders he has done,
his miracles, and the judgments.
1 CHRONICLES 16:12

I'm a hunter. My weapon is a camera, and I keep it loaded. In fact, five minutes ago, while going from one room to the other, I spotted a hawk on my patio, perched on the back of a chair. It's never been there before and may never be again. So, very quietly, I picked up my weapon with its 400mm zoom lens, crawled down the hallway, started to shoot, and clicked off maybe ten rounds on that single target. What a moment!

Two days ago, I picked off three hot-air balloons whooshing over my house. A month ago I shot the liftoff of the space shuttle Atlantis, and earlier this summer, I managed several close-up photos in a butterfly sanctuary.

I've snapped pictures of whales, wild animals in the bush, cat fights, foreign cities, autumn leaves, great horned owls, parties, weddings, children playing, lightning, snowfalls, family, friends, strangers. Many are framed and adorn my house. I consider almost every moment a "Kodak moment," to borrow a phrase. Why, I hardly go to the corner without my camera. What if I miss something? I couldn't stand it. Wherever I go, I'm in search of a memory.

I've journaled for many years because I want to remember meaningful times and people dear to me. I treasure these volumes more and more, and I count on them to reveal everything as it actually happened. They are a concise chronicle of my life.

When I turned sixty-five, one of my dearest friends gave me a memory book called "Remember When." She sent fifty blank pages to family members and friends and asked them to surprise me with the account of a time they remembered with me. There was a place to write and a spot to include a photo. I can't tell you what that gift means to me. When I opened it, I cried like a baby. The memories floated off those pages as my mind went a hundred different directions. It's a wonderful book. Maybe the best gift I've ever received.

And guest books? Let me tell you about those! I have the writings of my mom and dad (both now with the Lord), accounts of parties and holidays, and thank-you notes from countless friends. Each page is a wonderful memory captured on paper. Those books take me back to times of great joy.

Remembering is important to God. He encourages us to make memories. In Joshua 3–4, we read the account of the Israelites moving the ark of the covenant across the flooded Jordan River. After the water parted to allow the ark and the Israelites to cross, God commanded the leaders of the twelve tribes to take one stone each from the river and to place it where the priests had stood with the ark when they arrived safely on the other shore. "These stones are to be a memorial to the people of Israel forever" (Josh. 4:7). A stack of stones, believed to be the original one, stands on the bank of the Jordan today!

Scripture is replete with verses on remembering. We're encouraged to remember days of old, the wonders of God, the Sabbath, God's deeds and our struggles, our Creator, our youth, and that life is short. There are many commands *to remember.*

If you've not yet begun to create memories, start now. Load up your camera with film, fill that pen with ink, and capture the miracles and wonders that come your way. Surround yourself with whatever it takes to be reminded. God is faithful. Don't ever forget that.

Lord, help me to remember all the ways you lead me, bless me, keep me. May I be a repository of those memories and be quick to share them with others. They are the proof of your constant faithfulness. Thank you. Amen.

Don't Take My Word for It

I know your deeds, that you are neither cold nor hot.
I wish you were either one or the other!
So, because you are lukewarm—neither hot nor cold—
I am about to spit you out of my mouth.

REVELATION 3:15–16

A hillbilly walked into a novelty store. He saw a shiny thermos and asked the clerk what it was. The clerk replied, "It's a thermos. It keeps cold things cold and hot things hot." The hillbilly was so impressed he bought one.

He couldn't wait to show it off to his friends. At work the next day, he didn't have to wait long before one of his peers asked him what that shiny thing was.

The hillbilly replied, "It's a thermos. It keeps cold things cold and hot things hot."

His coworker asked him, "Well, what do you have in it now?"

The hillbilly proudly replied, "A Popsicle and two cups of coffee!"

I'm with the hillbilly. I like cold things cold, and hot things hot with no in-between. I'm all or nothing. I know what I like and what I don't. As a Southerner, I can eat my weight in fried okra but don't feed me hominy. As an opera lover, I'd lay down my life for Puccini's music but deliver me from Alban Berg. As a moviegoer, give me a sit-on-the-edge-of-my-chair psychological thriller but do not make me wade through some sappy, boy-meets-girl, girl-wears-cute-clothes, boy-marries-girl, couple-has-baby. Please!

You don't have to agree with me. It's often more fun when you don't; it sparks great conversation. I've worked for years to develop these opinions, and they define me.

That's one thing I love about Marilyn. She has her own thoughts, states her preferences, holds to her convictions, and when we differ, she doesn't try to change my mind. She lets me be me.

For instance, I love the Old Country Buffet restaurant in Palm Desert (where we both live), but Marilyn loathes it. The food caters to home-style cooking, honors senior citizen discounts, and one can go back to the trough as often as desired. It's inexpensive, all-you-can-eat, come-as-you-are. My kind of place! But Marilyn? No, thanks! If I want to go there, I have to find another hillbilly. Marilyn's opinion doesn't keep me from going; it just keeps me from going with her.

I remember a friend in my bygone days who could never make up her mind.

I'd ask, "Want to go to dinner?"

"It doesn't matter," she would say.

"Okay, let's go out. Afterward, how 'bout a movie?"

"Whatever you say."

"What would you like to see?"

"Whatever . . ."

That drove me crazy! I didn't mind deciding, but I never had the chance to know her. And you can be sure she didn't know herself.

Our choices validate us. They tell us who we are and convey to others where we stand. By not having personal convictions, my friend lacked strength of character. She went through life neither hot nor cold.

This becomes a serious problem when you go beyond music, movies, or meals to important issues like faith. I'm talking about a mind-set, a disposition toward life wherein Jesus Christ is your center, his Word is your standard, and his way your choice.

God requires a person to make choices—to be hot or cold, to know what you believe and why. I'm not suggesting we hold stubbornly or unreasonably to our own opinions. However, when it comes to biblical convictions or spiritual truth, we must take a stand. Wisdom, peace, courage, and joy characterize the people I know who do.

Father, help us make choices that please you. We don't want to be weak or stubborn. We want to be right on. Like you. Amen.

Start Dreaming

However, as it is written: "No eye has seen,
no ear has heard, no mind has conceived what
God has prepared for those who love him"—
but God has revealed it to us by his Spirit.

1 CORINTHIANS 2:9–10

Vision is when you see it and others don't. Faith is when you do it and others won't.

My friend Joanne had both. A superb interior designer, she could see a finished room in her mind's eye and know how to transform the image into reality.

My brother Chuck has both. Although he stuttered as a child, he envisioned himself speaking publicly. With the help of a drama coach, he memorized poetry to quit stuttering. It solved the problem.

My hairdresser Gloria has both. Discouraged by the absence of her husband, who worked in another city, she quit a more lucrative job, moved to where he was, and opened her own beauty supply store.

With vision and faith things can be done. There's a couplet by Goethe, which reads:

Whatever you can do, or dream you can, begin it.
Boldness has genius, power, and magic in it.

I well remember the months I debated about buying my home. There I was, sixty-two years old, never having owned property, taking out a thirty-year loan. Was I crazy? I wanted a spot to call my own. I imagined what it would be like, and with God as my partner, I stepped out in faith. With confidence in his leading, I boldly went forward. It seemed like magic. And now, what joy this place brings me!

One of the greatest by-products of believing in something and then going for it is joy. I've often said, "My favorite thing in life is doing something new while having a good time." That's the essence of joy. Webster defines it as "a very glad feeling; great pleasure; delight."

The psalmist says, "Delight yourself in the LORD and he will give you the desires of your heart" (Ps. 37:4). I believe this works two ways. We delight, or find joy, in the Lord, and he gives us our heart's desires. He puts his desires in our hearts and then fulfills them. I like that. No, I delight in that.

Let's get practical. Perhaps you have an idea of something you would like to do, but you're scared. You've never done anything like it before. Maybe the idea just won't go away. But it's outside your comfort zone, and you don't feel adequate for the task. Start to pray, "Lord, if this desire is from you, will you bring it to pass? Help me know where to start."

And then start. This is the faith part. Work hard. Do what makes sense to you. And then do the next thing. Ask the Lord whom to talk to who might help you. Talk with them. Ask him to keep discouragement from your door.

As you go, you'll begin to experience boldness because you started. You acted on your desire. You saw it in your mind and you began.

That is exactly how I started writing. Someone challenged me to write a book, and I was scared to death. But

God gave me the desire, he answered when I prayed, and it became a delight.

What has he given you the desire to do? You can do it. Conceive the idea and trust him. Then start. And, with delight, see what happens!

Give me your courage, Lord Jesus, to begin new things. Help me know what you want me to do, then enable me to do it joyfully. Amen.

A Quiet Life

[Pray] that we may lead a tranquil and quiet life
in all godliness and dignity.
1 TIMOTHY 2:2 NASB

I have a little plaque on my wall that reads, "Anything for a quiet life." I saw a bumper sticker today that suggested, "Honk if you love peace and quiet." I honked. I recently bought *The Little Book of Calm*. You get the picture. *Quiet, peace, calm* — even the words soothe my soul. That's why I love living in the desert.

The desert is a quiet place. Nobody hurries. My first week here I went to the grocery store, and right in the middle of the parking lot were two women, talking up a storm. Needing to park, I lightly beeped my horn and gestured for them to move to one side. Thinking I was waving, they simply smiled, waved back, and went right on talking. It didn't occur to them I would interrupt their conversation.

I love the community in the desert. Pat lives on my street, Patsy's a block away, and Marilyn, two. We take time to see each other, to have quiet time together, ignoring the hustle and bustle of life. I go by Marilyn's on my morning bike ride and drop off the newspaper. She offers me tea. We enjoy the visit. Pat and I go to our favorite place for lunch, just to talk. Patsy saunters by my house to compare notes on the book we're reading. My soul thrives here.

Just a couple of nights ago, an enormous, full moon appeared, and Mar and I sat on her back patio talking about prayer. We were there more than an hour. We didn't necessarily have the time; we chose to take it. When I got there, we both insisted we had only a few minutes. But neither of us wanted it to end.

The desert reminds me of my childhood in Texas: flat and dusty, with a big sky, frogs croaking, and crickets chirping. I take time to listen, and it's comforting. On hot summer evenings, I take a bubble bath and soak for a while, just to relax. I play beautiful music and sip a glass of cold lemonade.

But, when I want to completely retreat to the quiet life, it's not with my friends, the crickets, or the bath. It's with the Lord. Talk about a balm to my spirit. The joy and pleasure of speaking with the Lord is far superior to anything life on this earth affords. Through prayer I become centered and serene. When it's quiet and still, I sense the Lord comes near as I enter his presence.

I experience a silent symmetry when I'm alone with him that makes me calm. It strengthens me for the task at hand. In a culture where we all but worship activity and accomplishment, we can so easily miss time alone with him.

Remember what he said to Martha, who was such a little busy beaver, living, I guess, a loud and active life. He said, "Martha, Martha ... you are worried and upset about many things, but only one thing is needed. Mary has chosen what is better" (Luke 10:41–42). We know what Mary was doing: sitting calmly, quietly, at the Master's feet.

When you're tempted to run around and never stop, let me challenge you. Choose the better part. Be with your friends, relax a little, and most necessary, be with the Savior for a while. Ahh! Anything for a quiet life.

Father, give me the courage to stop occasionally and the grace to take time for necessary things. Amen.

Too Huge

Finally, brothers, whatever is true, whatever is noble,
whatever is right, whatever is pure, whatever is lovely,
whatever is admirable—if anything is excellent
or praiseworthy—think about such things.
PHILIPPIANS 4:8

I'll never forget Joanne DeGraw. She was unique, exceptional, and charming. Our friendship was extraordinary. When she died of cancer, which she battled bravely for seventeen years, something in me wanted to die too.

I loved Joanne. Texan by birth, she was highly educated, married to an attorney, and the mother of two. A former resident of France, she loved literature, art, theater, and music. She was an unparalleled interior designer.

When we met, I was renting an apartment. She promptly designed a house for me and said, if it ever became a reality, she would like to do the decorating. I was thrilled, and almost immediately we made plans. Although she died before I had my dream house, she lived to shepherd me through the process of purchasing furniture and appointments I needed for a leased condo.

Joanne had a great sense of humor in spite of the severity of her physical condition. Whether we were discussing the latest book we had read, an opera we had seen together, the Scripture, her children, or a project, she injected her flair for the funny in her sweet Southern twang.

I remember my excitement over finding a group of six teeny lamp shades I wanted to use on a chandelier in my dining room. They seemed perfect. When I showed them to Joanne, she said, "Why, Luci, those will never do!" Surprised, I asked why not. "They are too huge!" she responded. I couldn't imagine how anything less than two inches high could be too huge, but I trusted her judgment. On that, and everything else, she knew what she was doing.

A year before Joanne died, I visited her for four days. On the first morning, when I awakened, I found a pot of coffee, a gorgeous china cup, and this note on her personalized stationery: *Good morning, dear Luci, good morning to you. I am looking forward to spending a whole day with you. Enjoy the library in the peace of the morning, and the coffee while it's hot!*

During that precious time together we spent long days in front of a roaring fire, talking and laughing, reading aloud, eating, cooking, and chatting about dreams, joys, and regrets. On the third day she received the report that tumors for which she had been treated had, in fact, grown and metastasized into the liver. She hung up the phone, cried a few minutes, told me what had happened, and asked me to pray with her. Afterwards, out of the blue, she said, "I know a great bookstore in Grass Valley, Luci. Let's go over there and see what damage we can do, okay?" And away we went! The seriousness of her diagnosis didn't set the tone for our day; her indomitable spirit did. In spite of our sadness, the day was sweet, fun, and memorable.

Joanne could have made her suffering a time of emotional torment for herself and anguish for her loved ones, but she didn't. She decided instead to accept the path God gave her with courage, grace, and humor. Without denying her reality, she chose to think on what was excellent and praiseworthy.

When I look at the furniture she chose for the home I now own, I remember her joy of living and spirit of giving. I think, *Joanne DeGraw, your spirit was just too huge for this old world!*

Should you encounter bad news today, look within yourself. You'll find God's Spirit, who will enable you to accept graciously that which has been handed to you. Think on those parts of life that are lovely. For even in our saddest days, God is under that sorrow, holding us up.

Help me, Lord, to think on those things that bring honor to you. Give me joy in my circumstances so that my life will bring others joy instead of sadness. Amen.

Sweet, Wise, and Spiritual

We shall be like him, for we shall see him as he is.
1 JOHN 3:2

Okay, let's get this over with: I'm not exactly a dog lover. I can count on one hand the dogs I really like—and have fingers left over!

You wonder why? I didn't grow up in a family that *had* to have a dog. Instead, my older brother Orville raised dogs for a short period of time, and we were all subjected to his inordinate dedication to the task. That's probably what did us all in. One litter of barking dogs in your backyard suffices to make you think you've done enough for the dog world.

Also, I find it difficult to own something that has to be fed constantly. As a single, on-the-go professional, I've never had cats, goldfish, hamsters, babies, or birds. My only pets are plants. I don't mind offering food and water to any living thing on occasion, but *every* day?

However, recently I met a dog I liked. I was in New York, sitting with my friend Mary in a little coffee shop on Columbus Avenue, when in walked a rather slovenly woman with her dog. Mary, noting a striking resemblance between this dog and hers, began a conversation.

"What's your dog's name? He's so cute."

I looked up from my newspaper in an effort to appear Christian and friendly. I'll admit, I was a *bit* curious.

"His name's Ben," the woman said warmly.

The dog never moved an inch from his owner. He kept his gaze riveted on her. When she shifted, he shifted. When she waited, he waited. Perfectly behaved and still, he stood there as though transfixed until it was time to move forward in the line. He followed, close at heel. The woman paid for her coffee and muffin, then she and Ben turned to leave. As they neared our table on their way out, Mary and the New Yorker continued to visit.

Mary said, "He's so well-behaved."

The woman assured Mary he had been very well-trained, was always attentive to her, and obedient to every command. With a loving expression, she then reached down, petted Ben, and said to us, "Yes, Ben is sweet, wise, and spiritual."

With that, the woman and dog exited the café. Mary and I looked at each other, exchanged big smiles, and pondered the thought. "Spiritual?"

Remembering the incident later, I realized how wonderful it would be if my Master described me that way. Sweet, wise, and spiritual. You know, that's exactly what we become when we spend enough time with him. Those qualities, which are his, are reflected in us. The more faithful we are to him, the more attentive to his voice, the more obedient to his way, the more we become the kind of person we want to be. The kind of person he created us to be.

I like Ben. He's a good reminder of the value of keeping one's eyes on the Master. If I want to be sweeter, wiser, and even more spiritual, I need to spend time with the One who longs to lead me through this life. The One who wants to take me out in public and have others see the true quality of his life in me.

Lord, I desire to be more like you in every way. I know I can't begin to change in my own strength, so enable me by the power of your Spirit to reflect the sweetness and wisdom that come from spending time with you. May I value that more than anything. Amen.

Tongue-Tied

God loves old ordinary me, even or especially
at my most scared and petty and mean and obsessive.
Loves me; chooses me.
ANNE LAMOTT

When I moved to California twenty-five years ago, I often went with Marilyn to hear her speak. One fall day we were heading home when we both spotted a sign: FRESH APPLE PIE. TURN HERE. We did.

There was quite a crowd gathered in line for pie. Among those waiting was a large, tough-looking, loud-mouthed woman wearing a uniform. She ordered several pieces of pie. I assumed she was going into the bush to chow down with the militia. We both commented on how loud and rude she was, yelling at several little Boy Scouts who were enjoying themselves too much on her shift.

After getting our pie, we joined about thirty people, all strangers, and enjoyed chatting, eating, and drinking coffee. Suddenly, Loud Mouth came into the center of the circle, holding a piece of pie and yelling, "DAVIIIIIID! DAVID! Get over here right now!" All eyes turned as David, about seven, hurried up to her with his arms out to take the pie.

"When I call you, you answer me. DO YOU HEAR ME?" She proceeded to hit David in the head, knocking his cap off and his pie into the dirt.

I was stunned. Horrified. Speechless.

We all stopped eating, talking . . . breathing. Momentarily, out of the silence, we heard a lone, stern voice say, "You hit that child one more time, and you'll have to deal with me."

I was dumbfounded. It was Marilyn; tender, gracious, unarmed Marilyn. *Are you crazy?* I thought. *Loud Mouth is going to make mincemeat out of you.*

Let me remind you, this was twenty-five years ago. Child abuse was not the issue it is today. I had never seen a child abused in a public place, and I'd certainly never seen anyone defend or protect a stranger's child. I was sure Marilyn was going to be decked, if not destroyed.

But nothing happened. Marilyn's gaze was fixed on the woman, the woman stared back, everyone in the crowd looked at each other, and I crawled under a rock, mortified. You see, I believe in minding my own business. And that's my preference for everyone. I was concerned about the child, but I was more concerned about seeing my dear friend clobbered in broad daylight.

No further words were exchanged, but a heavy pall hung over the place. As we began to disperse, various people came up to Marilyn to say, "I admire you for doing that." Or, "I never could have stood up to that woman, but it was great that you did." Some folks simply said, "Thank you."

The more I listened to these comments, the more conflicted I felt inside. I'd chosen to do what comes naturally to me. I'd decided to say nothing. I'd even wanted Marilyn to stay silent. But I was wrong. Dead wrong. I didn't have the courage to openly defend that little boy even though I knew his scout leader was brutally off base. I was afraid of what might happen if I spoke up . . .

if anybody spoke up. I was afraid of what would happen to me. My apprehension struck me mute.

There resides in the heart of every believer little pockets of fear. For some of us it's cowardice. For others, it's timidity. Although we know the Savior gives courage and power, sometimes we feel safer in our little pocket than in his big provision. So we cower inside, afraid to be bold. We permit our human frailty to stand in the way of his strength.

Amazingly though, God has grace for this kind of behavior. He understands our weaknesses. Just because Marilyn spoke up and I didn't, that doesn't mean he likes her better than he does me. I take comfort in that because even in my most unbecoming, inept, self-loathing moments, God still loves me with all his heart. When my weakness prevails rather than his strength, he doesn't condemn me. He doesn't compare me to Marilyn. Now when I come face-to-face with my less-than-perfect behavior, instead of condemning or comparing, I'm learning to lean on him and pray, "Lord, make me more like you. When I want to retreat, give me your courage." He longs to, and he does.

To me this fact is one of the most remarkable aspects of God's character. He chooses me because he *wants* to. And he changes me. Makes me more like I wish I were. More like him.

But you, O Lord, are a compassionate and gracious God, slow to anger, abounding in love and faithfulness. Turn to me and have mercy on me; grant your strength to your servant.

PSALM 86:15–16

Mothers I Have Known

But we were gentle among you,
like a mother caring for her little children.
1 THESSALONIANS 2:7

Beth is the most wonderful mother. Granted, her children are still babies, but she is off to a great start. She has finished a master's program in psychology, traveled in Europe, worked in a drug rehabilitation clinic, and lived an adventuresome life. Yet, her real colors shine when she is with her two boys. She was *made* for motherhood. And why not?

You see, I know her mother, Marilyn, with whom I've been friends since Beth was five. I've watched as Marilyn gave Beth love, affection, discipline, a fun childhood, and wise mentoring. Marilyn encouraged Beth to be her best, introduced her to Jesus Christ at a young age, cheered her growth and development as an individual, and helped to provide her a good education. Marilyn was a caring, strong, unique mother, and one I admired greatly. But why wouldn't she be?

You see, I knew *her* mother, Elizabeth. Beth's grandmother was one of the most interesting women I've ever known. Quiet and reserved, she had a ready wit and smile. A wonderful listener, she was always eager to spend time with her daughter and her grandchildren, listening to their joys or woes. Her love of reading and learning was passed down to the next generation, then the next. Elizabeth established a pattern for mothering that Marilyn emulated, and now, Beth.

As a single person with no children, let me say I believe life's highest calling is motherhood. An endeavor like no other, it demands a sense of selflessness that must be renewed every day.

I enjoy watching my friends interact with their children. It's fascinating. Shortly after meeting Sheila, she said being a mother is the great leveler of humanity. (Her son, Christian, is now four.)

"On Monday morning, Christian doesn't care that I'm tired from speaking all weekend," she explained. "He wants to go to his swimming lesson and wants me to take him. So I get up and go. It's as simple as that." (I guess he doesn't know she's Sheila Walsh!)

I remember an article in the *LA Times* about the California Mother of the Year.* Her name is Barbara Hoche. She has three daughters. Wanting to be actively involved in their lives, she was their room mother, a PTA officer, a Brownie troop leader, and a Sunday school teacher. She escorted the girls to movies and plays and took them shopping.

Mothers engage in these activities all the time, but Barbara Hoche is remarkable because she is confined to a wheelchair. Mrs. Hoche was hit by an automobile as a twenty-year-old student and was paralyzed. She's now in her seventies.

The article was filled with high praise from her daughters: "When we were little, Mother would lay us across her lap and off she'd go through the house." Or, "When we were older, she'd take us shopping, and if we

---

*"Celebrating Being Alive," *Los Angeles Times,* March 30, 1998.

got tired, we'd sit on her footrests and she'd scoot across the mall."

Fluent in Bulgarian, she served as a translator in the 1984 Olympics. Her thirty-six-year-old daughter said, "I got comments all the time from friends saying they wished they had a mother like mine."

You may not be a mother, but you have a mother. Did you know the only one of the Ten Commandments that carries a promise with it is the one about honoring your parents? "Honor your father and your mother, so that you may live long in the land the LORD your God is giving you" (Exod. 20:12). God blesses with longevity those who hold their mothers in high regard. Call your mother today and say, "I love you. I'm glad you're my mom."

Those were the last words I said to my mother on the night she died suddenly at the age of sixty-three. The day I'm writing this devotional is her birthday. She would have been ninety-one. I'm glad I called.

Heavenly Father, with tremendous gratitude I thank you for mothers. Strengthen them, Lord, for the enormous responsibility placed upon their shoulders. In Jesus' name. Amen.

Here a Verse, There a Verse

Do your best to present yourself to God as one approved,
a workman who does not need to be ashamed
and who correctly handles the word of truth.

2 TIMOTHY 2:15

One evening at dinner with a group of Dallas Seminary students, I was exchanging favorite Bible verses with them. A third-year student said, "Mine is 1 Chronicles 26:18."

I couldn't imagine what that was, so I quickly asked, "What is it?"

"'At Parbar westward, four at the causeway, and two at Parbar.'"

I thought for a moment, not wanting to seem like a dunce in the presence of a theologian. Finally, I had to admit it made no sense to me. "Is that *it?*" I questioned. "What does it *mean?*"

His answer was classic. "Who knows?" We all laughed hysterically.

I was reminded of the times I've talked about the favorite verse of single women: "If any man will come after me, let him . . ." (Matt. 16:24 KJV). Now, mind you, if you read the verse in its entirety, the meaning changes drastically. But take it out of context, and it makes a very different point.

Once I printed a verse from Matthew 23 on a little watercolor I painted for a friend. The portion of the verse I used says, " . . . You travel over land and sea to win a single convert . . ." (v. 15). That verse fits precisely the message I wanted to convey to my soul-winning friend. However, in proper context, you realize in that passage Jesus actually was condemning the Pharisees' action. He called them hypocrites because they were converting people to their own pharisaical ways, *not* the gracious ways of God.

These harmless exchanges of verses' meanings are fun, but sometimes it goes way beyond humor. How many times have we heard people *seriously* quote Scripture or use a verse to their own advantage rather than for its intended meaning? They *believe* what is lifted out of context, and that's dangerous!

God imparts his commands, plans, and ideas with specificity. There's no mixed message in what he's saying. But when I believe bits and pieces of Scripture, removed from their frame of reference, I run the chance of living in a dream world, waiting for things to happen according to my preference. Isaiah 55:8–11 (TLB) says:

> This plan of mine is not what you would work out, neither are my thoughts the same as yours! For just as the heavens are higher than the earth, so are my ways higher than yours, and my thoughts than yours. As the rain and snow come down from heaven and stay upon the ground to water the earth, and cause the grain to grow and to produce seed for the farmer and bread for the hungry, so also is my Word. I send it out and it always produces fruit. It shall accomplish all I want it to, and prosper everywhere I send it.

Oh, my, that's beautiful and ever so true! Become a student of Scripture. Know what it teaches. Believe what it says. Understand what it means. Impart its truth to others. When we share the Bible with others, we are giving them *life* . . . wonderful words of *life!* We're not just making suggestions for living; we're offering individuals a new way to think, act, feel, and live. It's not here a verse, there a verse. *In context,* it's a new way to understand life. God's way.

Sing them over again to me, Lord, wonderful words of life. Let me more of their beauty see, wonderful words of life. Amen.

At Your Service

O LORD, God of Abraham, Isaac and Israel, let it be known
today that you are God in Israel and that I am your servant
and have done all these things at your command.

1 KINGS 18:36

About my purse. I only carry what is absolutely essential in there. Only what I really need. Or might need. In addition to typical items one might expect such as a billfold, checkbook, notepad, and coin purse, I carry other important stuff. For example: hand cream; tissues; instant antibacterial hand gel; electronic organizer; and leather cases for postcards, stamps, credit cards, pens, Post-It notes, and sunglasses. Oh, and I have to have my Day Timer, glasses cleanser, and a small black satchel crammed full of other important paraphernalia such as lipstick, mirror, toothpicks, nail file, international clock, hole punch, a Swiss Army knife with its twenty-six "tools," and a booklet that tells folks how to accept the Lord. I don't carry the kitchen sink, but I do have everything it takes to repair one. Okay, so I have back pain. I also have what I need when I need it.

If you think my purse is full, try looking in my dresser drawers! Barbara Johnson sent me a handheld mirror not long ago, which I store in one of my drawers. Every time I open that drawer, the mirror lets out a wolf whistle. No matter how bad I look or how low I feel, here comes this wonderful "woeeee-weoooo." Makes me perk right up. That whistle always cheers an otherwise dull day. Other drawers have equally fascinating treasures. I'm bonded to my stuff, and everybody knows it.

I like things that serve my needs. And I want access to them conveniently, immediately, and continuously.

Recently, I opened two small packets of Bayer aspirin. Inside was a flat, folded paper cup. When you pressed its tiny sides, it opened so you could put water inside and drink from it. I was ecstatic. I put that adorable cup right in my purse. I might need it sometime. Printed on it were the words, "Another innovative idea for 'people on the go' from Mechanical Servants, Inc."

How clever. Somebody's newfangled idea to meet a need. My kitchen is full of such gadgets. Knife sharpeners. Mixers. Bread machines. Blenders. Cheese graters. Lemon squeezers.

And the bathroom! Toothbrushes, night-lights, multi-spray showerheads, magnifying mirrors, and mobile phone. Every day we call on our mechanical servants, and we want them *now*.

I looked up the word "servant" in my concordance and found it's used more than four hundred times in Scripture. Of course, those servants were in the human rather than mechanical form, but the idea is the same. They did the bidding of the one with whom they were aligned. And repeatedly God commended them. Abraham was called the servant of God. And Moses. And David. In fact, David, as a servant of the Lord, wrote in Psalm 119:124–25:

> Deal with your servant according to your love
> and teach me your decrees.
> I am your servant; give me discernment
> that I may understand your statutes.

I want to be God's servant. When he asks me to do something, I want to be responsive. Instantly and always. My desire is to be as ready and convenient for his use as my stuff is for mine. He has equipped me with all the tools I need to be used for his purpose. There's nothing mechanical about it.

Father, give me the spirit of a servant, a heart that is more giving, loving, and attentive to the needs of others than to those of myself. Will you help me with that? Amen.

The Rabbi and I

The grass withers and the flowers fall,
but the word of our God stands forever.
ISAIAH 40:8

We were practically twins. He was dressed in black from head to toe, as was I. He carried black luggage, just as I did. He was reading a book. Me too. The primary difference was he had a long, gray, untrimmed beard that hung over the front of his coat. *That* I couldn't match.

We were sitting in the waiting room of the Palm Springs Airport anticipating our departure to Dallas–Ft. Worth, killing time before we boarded the plane. The morning was cold. Early February. After scrutinizing the surroundings, I opened my book. It was *Psalms,* a modern translation by Eugene Peterson. My twin opened his book too . . . the Old Testament, in Hebrew. I noticed out of the corner of my eye the hardback spine was worn and tattered and the pages well marked. My book was new and paperback. It cracked when I opened it.

I watched him ever so intently as he pored over the Scriptures, his aging fingers underlining the words he read. Suddenly we were more than dressed alike. We were kindred spirits. I too had spent years with God's Word . . . maybe not as many as he, but at least five decades. The Scriptures gave direction to my parents as I was growing up, guidance to us as a family, credibility to my life choices. I've memorized and believed Bible verses from my earliest remembrance.

Obviously, this rabbi also knew where to go to hear God's voice. Coming from such diverse backgrounds, we shared this common bond. Because the Scriptures never change, the truth is available to anyone anywhere. When we open God's Word, we hear Yahweh speak — the personal God of the Hebrew people who declared his existence to them so many centuries ago.

I knew nothing about this stranger in the airport except that we looked alike and had the same taste in books. Our paths crossed in a moment of time, and I'll probably never see him again. However, the memory of that encounter lives in my mind because of its significance.

God's Word will stand forever. It is more than an Old and New Testament compiled into sixty-six books that constitute a divine library. It is a source of guidance, strength, encouragement, and comfort, available every day of our lives. From the ancient sands of Israel to the shores of the New World, the Bible always has been an incredible story of faith and sacrifice. Even when it was banned, burned, and barred from the reading public, God's truth could not be crushed or stopped.

The other night I picked up *Psalms,* and as I was reading, I thought of the bearded rabbi. I remembered the day in the airport and the sweetness of that scene. I wondered if he was somewhere reading the same words as I:

> God, teach me lessons for living
> so I can stay the course.
> Give me insight so I can do what you tell me —
> My whole life one long, obedient response.
> Guide me down the road of your commandments;
> I love traveling this freeway!
>
> PSALM 119:33–35 MSG

Take a few minutes today to spend with Yahweh. Find the comfort and guidance you need from God's words of direction for that disturbing circumstance in your life. His words are there, and they're written *just for you.*

You are the God of Abraham, Isaac, and Jacob, and you are no less my God today than you were for them. Thank you for your provision when I need it most. Thank you for thinking of everything. Help my life be "one long, obedient response." Amen.

He Knows My Name

The watchman opens the gate for him,
and the sheep listen to his voice.
He calls his own sheep by name and leads them out.

JOHN 10:3

The minute I saw the book I started dreaming. When Dr. Billy Graham's autobiography, *Just as I Am,* was published, I longed to give a leather-bound copy to my friend Ney Bailey. Ney had trusted the Lord with Dr. Graham during the 1951 Shreveport, Louisiana, Crusade. Not just her spiritual father, Dr. Graham is also one of her heroes in the faith. I could think of nothing more delightful than for her to receive a copy of his book, personally inscribed by him to her.

So my quest began. I wanted it for a Christmas present, and I went after it like Indiana Jones pursued the lost ark.

First I wrote Zondervan to obtain a leather-bound edition. Then I called Dr. Graham's office. The book came quickly, but I received no response to my call for an autograph. I wrote a letter explaining how desperate I felt and how important this was. Four months passed. Nothing! I wrote again. Finally, a very sweet letter of apology came, advising me there would be no autograph due to Billy Graham's ill health and his busy schedule. The unsigned book was enclosed.

I was crushed. Tempted to give up, I kept thinking, *It's not over till it's over. And, Lord, it ain't over!*

Less than a week later, I was having dinner with friends. We were engaged in enjoyable conversation about nothing in particular when Sheila Walsh casually mentioned her friend Ruth Graham.

Ruth Graham? I thought. *As in . . . Billy Graham?* I was quiet, but my heart raced. Maybe my friend Sheila could lead me to the Holy Grail. "Ahem, Sheila," I said casually, "not to change the subject, but how well do you know Ruth Graham?"

Sheila popped back in her Scottish brogue, "She's one of my best friends. I'm *nuts* about 'er."

I took a deep breath, trying to contain my excitement. Then I explained the whole thing to Sheila. "Give me the book," she said, "I'll see wha' I cun do."

She went right to work on it, sending the book with a personal note to Billy Graham. I prayed.

Three weeks passed. Nothing! *Then . . .* just before I was to be with Ney for Christmas, Sheila called, yelling into the phone, "Luci, the book came. It's wonderful. Listen to what he said . . ." It was incredible. Sheila cried. I cried. And everybody who had been praying cried.

But *nobody* cried like Ney. When Christmas morning came and she unwrapped that book, the tears began. They continued as she read aloud:

> To Ney Bailey,
> God bless you always.
> Billy Graham
> Philippians 1:6

Ney exclaimed, "He knows my name! He knows my *name!*" It was an enormously gratifying moment worth all the waiting.

Philippians 1:6 says, "He who began a good work in you will carry it on to completion." That was such a reality to us that day. God had begun his work in Ney's young heart in the Shreveport stadium years ago. Through the years, he had been faithful to continue. Ney had grown. And been used by him to lead thousands to Christ.

I was reminded through the whole scenario with the book that God is interested in the tiniest things in the world. He cares about us and what we consider important. He gives us the desires of our hearts. He completes what he begins. He knows us by name.

Lord, how I praise you for seeing us through to the end. You ask us to trust you. You call us by name. What a joy it is that you know us personally. Amen.

When Words Matter

Listen, O heavens, and I will speak; hear, O earth,
the words of my mouth. Let my teaching fall like rain
and my words descend like dew, like showers on new grass,
like abundant rain on tender plants.

DEUTERONOMY 32:1–2

All I wanted was something to take off the chill. I was
in the Cincinnati airport with my dear friend Ann
Wright. Feeling rather cold, I suggested, "How 'bout a
nice cup of hot chocolate?" We headed toward a little coffee bar I'd spotted when we deplaned.

We moseyed over to the counter and asked the woman
for two cups of hot chocolate. With a smile she said, "We
don't serve hot chocolate here, ma'am, but right over there
you'll find some. Ask for 'Christine Miller.' They're the best."

Now, I heard *nothing* about Christine Miller. But that
was *exactly* what Ann swears she heard. *I* felt sure the
waitress encouraged us to *"ask for skim milk."* Since my
companion was older, wiser, and more experienced, I
took her word for it.

Ann found a table for two as I ordered two Christine
Millers. "Christine *what?*" was the incredulous response.

"Christine Millers! I understand that's the best hot
chocolate. Two please."

Well, you should have seen the blank expression on
that poor woman's face. She verbally stumbled around,

drew back from the counter, peered underneath in search of something, and finally responded, "I'm sorry, ma'am. All we have is Carnation." I felt sure she thought we had already been drinking somewhere else.

Holding back my laughter, I muttered, "That's fine. I'll take it; no problem" and went to find the perpetrator of this whole mess. There she sat, patiently waiting for her Christine Miller. I hated to tell her she was having a plain old Carnation hot chocolate!

Ann and I have laughed about that for months. We've told it to others with relish. Who cares if clerks in the Cincinnati airport consider us complete idiots? No harm done. The joke was on us. As I've heard Gloria Gaither say, "Don't hear what I say . . . hear what I mean."

Wouldn't *that* be great? Sometimes, though, our words are of utmost importance. Saying the right thing is crucial.

Last Christmas I was cruising along the Chilean coast, when suddenly we spotted a wrecked ship jutting out of the water, high and dry. The captain informed us this was the "Santa Leonora" which, on her maiden voyage in 1964, went aground due to a misunderstood command. The captain and the helmsman had been engaged in conversation when they transited "shoal pass." On completion of their talk, the captain simply said, "Alright, pilot." The pilot responded with a full right rudder, causing the ship to veer sharply to starboard and mount the shallows at full speed, where she still rests today. The captain had said a casual "alright," but the pilot had heard the instruction, "all right," which meant something very different. The result was deadly.

God speaks to us clearly. He means what he says. When he says he'll provide, we can count on that. When he promises peace, wisdom, strength, or comfort, they are ours. God imparts his word and keeps it. His words matter! I find tremendous comfort in that.

Sit down with a cup of hot chocolate today and enjoy his Word. Try a Christine Miller, alright?

Help me to believe you completely, Lord. Remind me you are never confused or distracted, but what you say you mean. Reveal in my own life the truth of this every day so my faith gets stronger and stronger. Amen.

One-Way Street

> I believe that God did lean down to become
> Man in order that we could reach up to Him.
> MALCOLM MUGGERIDGE

I love words. Words, and their meanings, are fascinating to me. When Malcolm Muggeridge says, "God did lean down to become Man," I am struck by the power of his words. They convey the incredible thought that deity and humanity are one, in Christ. A profound truth, simply stated.

There's also something fun about playing with words. If you've seen the "Sniglets" calendar, you know what I mean. For example, in "Sniglets," *profanitype* is a word that means "special symbols used by cartoonists to replace swear words." Or, how about *umbroglio*—"any conflict with an umbrella on a windy day." I also like *Jemimites*. These are extremely tiny pancakes formed from the batter that falls off the ladle.

Some of my favorite authors are those who do original gymnastics with words or phrases. The witty and erudite Dorothy Parker was once asked to make a sentence with the word "horticulture." In a flash she shot back, "You can lead a horticulture, but you can't make her think." Or how about Molly Ivins, a journalist from Texas. She coined the word "fize" . . . as in, "Fize younger I'd move to Europe" or, "Fize a rich woman I'd drive a better car."

I've been known to conveniently create a few words (or definitions of words) myself when the ones I had just wouldn't do. I remember one summer making a big sign for a Fourth of July party at Marilyn's house. Her daughter, Beth, and I worked on it for days. It was red, white, and blue, of course, and it stretched across the entire backyard. In big block letters we spelled out, LETH TAKE JULY BY FOURTH.

Then there was the Christmas when I wanted to make a card for my dear friend Mary Graham to commemorate the season in a unique and special way. She had just returned from a mission trip to Russia, so I drew a Russian Orthodox church, complete with cupolas, on the front of the card. Under it I planned to write "Merry Christmas" in Russian. But when I searched my books, the library, dictionaries, etc., I could not find out how to say "Merry Christmas" in that language.

When my quest proved fruitless, I didn't give up. I simply found a short Russian word followed by a long one (looked like Merry Christmas to me!) and used them. Mary didn't read Russian, so she'd never know. The words I chose actually meant "One-Way Street." As I printed them under the church in Cyrillic script, it hit me: "One-Way Street" was a very appropriate way to say Merry Christmas! So, I added this note to the card:

> Actually, I wanted this to say Merry Christmas in Russian, but I couldn't find it. So it says One-Way Street, which is sort of the same thing when you think about it. The birth of Christ is the One Way to peace, hope, joy, laughter . . . all that Christmas means. May Christmas be all of that and more to you, dearest Mary — a one-way street to happiness.

We've had so much fun with that card. And on blustery December days we smile at total strangers and say with a big grin, "One-Way Street!"

"For God so loved the world that he gave his one and only Son, that whoever believes in him shall not perish but have eternal life" (John 3:16). You couldn't make up better words than those! They are your one-way street to life. A gift for all eternity.

Fize you, I'd believe it.

Jesus answered, "I am the way and the truth and the life. No one comes to the Father except through me."
JOHN 14:6

Momo's Magic

Man is born broken. He lives by mending.
The grace of God is glue.

EUGENE O'NEILL

My maternal grandmother was wonderful. Sometimes I wish she were around today because she'd be up for anything fun or enterprising or adventuresome. We called her "Momo," and she loved the nickname.

Extremely musical (having taught piano for more than thirty years), Momo sang in the church choir, was a big-time party-giver, and an inveterate storyteller. She never missed anybody's birthday, kept journals and scrapbooks all her long life, and insisted on bringing a huge bunch of folk home for a big dinner after church almost every Sunday. "What's one more mouth to feed?" she'd say. "We'll just add another bean to the pot."

Momo's indomitable sense of humor saw her through life's tough situations and brought joy to her four children and many grandchildren. I still miss her even though she's been with the Lord forty-nine years.

On my tenth birthday, Momo gave me a new shiny blue bicycle—my first. I was ecstatic. My brothers each had one, so naturally I wanted one too. Envisioning myself with an inherent riding ability, I was outside at dawn's early light to engage in what was going to become "my sport." I lifted my leg to get on my new steed. Just then the wheels moved forward, and I fell. Clearly, this bike-riding business looked a lot easier than it was.

I tried again. And again. There was something about moving forward while staying seated that seemed like patting your head and rubbing your stomach at the same time. I couldn't get the hang of it. After an hour of failure to even get on the seat, I threw the bike against the big oak tree and stormed inside.

Later I tried again and the results were much the same. The bike simply didn't want to be ridden. After several more attempts I finally mounted it, wobbled about two feet, only to have my pants leg catch in the drive chain. Falling off once again, I furiously tugged at the cloth and the chain, getting oil on my hands and a rip in my pants. Huffing and puffing, I threw the bike against the tree. Again.

After several days, the bike and tree were quite bonded, and I was a living hornet's nest. That bicycle hated me . . . and the feeling was mutual. A week into this standoff, Momo asked how I was progressing and said she'd like to watch me ride. Little did she know her gift was now a crooked heap of metal, with wheels out of alignment, bent frame, scuffed handlebars, and dirty seat that was almost twisted off. Uh-oh.

Defeated, I pushed the bike over to Momo's house and told her how bad I felt because I couldn't ride . . . that I was a failure, and was sorry for the mess I'd made. I cried and asked her to forgive me. She looked at the bike (if I remember correctly, her eyes did sort of roll), then at me, and said, "Honey, anything's hard when you first start out, but be patient. You'll get the hang of it before long; then it'll be fun. Don't give up."

That encouragement from my grandmother was just the inspiration I needed to press on. The next day I actually rode about five minutes without falling. The bike and I were both wobbling along, but I hung in there. There was something about Momo believing in me that held me on that wobbly seat and propelled me forward. I've been an avid bike rider ever since.

Sometimes God gives us gifts that are hard for us to enjoy or appreciate so we misuse them. He graces us with a day of rest apart from the turmoil, but instead of enjoying his soothing presence we fill the quiet with television or mindless activity. He sends a friend to support us when we're blue, but because it isn't exactly who we want to be with we brush her off and miss the gift. He gives us an opportunity to forgive, but we cling to our bitterness and hold on to the grudge. He offers us a chance to be taught something new, but we're too proud to learn. The list goes on.

We need to recognize how often we mistrust the Lord and reject his gracious gifts because they're not on our terms. We can tell him how disappointed we are. He meets us in our honesty, mends us with his grace, and pours the oil of his love all over us. Even if things are still not in perfect alignment, we're able to move forward.

This is what the LORD says, he who made the earth, the LORD who formed it and established it — the LORD is his name: "Call to me and I will answer you and tell you great and unsearchable things you do not know."
JEREMIAH 33:2–3

Snaggletooth

When we understand that God has called us individually
by name, it profoundly alters the way we live.
MOTHER ANGELICA

One of my favorite television commercials has no words. A young woman walks into a shop and admires a bathing suit on a mannequin. With a look of self-satisfaction, she picks up a suit like it, disappears into a dressing room, throws her own clothes over the door, then, after a couple seconds, lets out a bloodcurdling scream. It's a powerhouse endorsement of the diet the commercial recommends. I laugh every time I see it as I munch away on my Snickers.

How many times do we look in the mirror and find no words to express what we see? The mirror talks. We scream. Thelma has a good idea. She says, "I'm fully clothed when I look in the mirror 'cause I don't want nuthin' talkin' back to me." Well put!

Recently I had a little screaming fit in front of my bathroom mirror. The dentist had attached a temporary cap on one of my permanent front teeth, which he had earlier filed away to a tiny squared-off yellow stub. That night when I was brushing, the cap fell off into the sink and disappeared down the drain.

At first, with the movement of the toothbrush and a mouthful of toothpaste, I couldn't tell it was gone. I just had a virtual sense of vacancy. Then, running my tongue across my front teeth, I felt nothing more than that stub. The cap was gone. For good. Forever. Forsooth! (Actually, I thought something else, but you don't want to know.)

I smiled into the mirror, then screamed. In short, I panicked. And I rarely panic. Generally I'm very calm, and little makes me lose my cool. But losing my tooth? Well, I lost my cool. I moaned, groaned, whimpered, and wailed. (It's hard to do all that at the same time, but I managed.) I looked in the mirror, hoping a second glance might bring back the tooth, but saw only that awful, gaping hole.

While pacing the hallway, I asked the Lord to take my life. I prayed for the return of Christ. This gaping hole in my mouth was a serious problem. I was leaving at dawn the next morning for Cincinnati.

With an unsteady hand I eventually dialed my dentist at home, told him I had to speak to 15,000 women at a conference the next day, and had no front tooth. I just knew he'd say, "Oh, honey, I understand. You come to the office right now, and I'll fix everything." But he didn't. He promised to meet me the next morning before my flight.

The next *morning?* He might as well have said in my next lifetime! Needless to say, I had a restless night envisioning the most embarrassing moment of my life surrounded by a sea of laughing women.

The next day Dr. Baumann and I both showed up early and the replacement was done. A very caring, kind man, he looked at me and said (with both fists and several tons of metal in my mouth), "Luci . . . what if you had to speak with that stub showing? You're still the same person inside, aren't you?"

That'th eathy for you to thay, pal. But, you know what? It's true. No matter how different I look on the outside,

I'm still me behind that snaggletooth. And I'll be me when I'm completely toothless one day! God, have mercy.

Sometimes the hardest thing in life is being ourselves. We so want to be somebody else. For years I sang with the Dallas Opera chorus, playing the part of other people. It was great. I wore wigs, corsets, fake eyelashes, heavy makeup, and costumes in order to become a waitress or a factory worker, nun, courtesan, schoolteacher, soldier, witch, dancer, or lady-in-waiting. Whatever was called for, I became that. Interestingly, even my friends in the chorus used to say, "My favorite thing about all this is that I don't have to be me."

The next time you stand in front of a mirror and want to scream, try to remember that God made that face. That smile. Those big eyes, crooked teeth, and chubby cheeks. You are his creation, called to reflect him. Spiritual transformation doesn't come from a diet program, a bottle, a makeover, or a mask. It comes from an intimate relationship with the Savior. Because of his gracious nature, he looks beyond our snaggletoothed grin and appreciates us for who we really are. So we can too.

The LORD does not look at the things man looks at. Man looks at the outward appearance, but the LORD looks at the heart.

1 SAMUEL 16:7

My Backyard Sanctuary

With God's enablement live this day to the full—
as if it were your last day on earth.

CHUCK SWINDOLL

For six months the plants on my patio have been either dead or dying. I've heard their little throats rattle each time I walk outside. Having had my fill of this I decided two weeks ago to spend whatever time it took to bring new life to the patio.

I went to the nursery, bought luxuriant flowering plants, potting soil, and pony packs. Four days, two blistered hands, and one achy-breaky back later, I have something akin to Monet's garden at Giverny—though on a smaller scale. I even bought a new patio chair and table so I could enjoy my garden in the cool of the evenings. It is one spiffy spot and brings pure pleasure and sheer satisfaction. Every day I deadhead plants, encouraging each plant to blossom anew by removing the old, faded flowers. I water, study growth, visit with the little blossoms, and cut bouquets for the house. That's what I was doing this morning when I heard a whooshing sound.

Looking up, I saw right over my head a huge, colorful hot-air balloon. Oh. My. Gosh. For a minute I thought it might land on the patio. I ran in, grabbed my camera, and was back in a flash, taking pictures. Somebody from the basket yelled down, "Good morning!" *Well, I guess!* Then more balloons came. And more. In all, there were a dozen filling the sky. My own private show. Nobody was out there to see them but my trusty little camera and me. I shot a whole roll of film, just like that. And it all happened before 7 A.M. What a way to start a day.

When was the last time you walked outside and looked around? Or up? Or under? Or through the leaves and limbs of a tree to see what was there? There's something, I can tell you for sure. It's waiting to be discovered and enjoyed—by you.

The backyard of the house where I used to live is a perfect example. It had an enormous spreading sycamore tree with branches reaching into the next county. A majestic, hovering thing! I was standing under it one day talking with a friend when she said quietly, "Turn around very slowly, Luci. Look up in the tree. On a low branch is a huge horned owl." Neither of us could believe our eyes. We stared. He stared back, unblinking. What a magnificent moment. Keeping my eyes on the owl, I whispered, "Whatever you do, honey, don't let that owl leave before I get a picture. I'll be right back."

Because I keep my camera loaded with film and just inside the doorway, I was able to snatch it and get several good shots before the owl moved, blinked, or thought twice. Actually, he stayed there most of the day, claiming that branch for himself. He was a wise old bird who knew what he wanted. I named him Wizard. It became almost a daily routine for me to watch for Wizard with my binoculars out my bedroom window.

One morning about 7:45, a fascinating drama unfolded in that tree. A red-shouldered hawk decided he wanted Wizard's spot and swooped down with lots of "kyaah, kyaah, kyaahs." Joining this audible fray were black grackles, mockingbirds, and a pair of outnumbered house wrens. I'd never heard such a racket. It went on for five or ten minutes and I witnessed the whole thing from my window. That night in my journal I recorded it, with drawings of the birds and the tree. It was September 18, 1993.

Then two months later something entirely different but equally as fascinating happened. My journal entry:

> You're not going to believe this, Journal, but I was opening my bedroom shutters this morning at 6:30 on a dark, rainy day . . . it was just dawn . . . and I saw a big dog (without a leash) on my back grassy knoll. It was loping or kind of stalking. Strange looking. Big tail. Suddenly, I realized it was a coyote. I watched it with my binoculars until it finally wandered off down by Gestapo's house.

("Gestapo" is the name I gave the neighborhood creep. He patrolled the out-of-doors—never finding anything pleasurable as far as I know.)

Check out your own backyard. Keep your eyes peeled. God's gracious gifts are everywhere—wrapped in a bird's nest, or popping out of the ground, or flying overhead. Take a picture. Write it down. Make a drawing. Enjoy!

Give thanks to the LORD for his unfailing love and his wonderful deeds.

PSALM 107:8

Sundays with Edna

When grace is joined with wrinkles, it is adorable.
There is an unspeakable dawn in happy old age.
VICTOR HUGO

Even though (according to Abigail Van Buren) folks are worth a fortune in old age "with silver in their hair, gold in their teeth, stones in their kidneys, lead in their feet and gas in their stomachs," aging is a journey we don't eagerly anticipate. As Henry James says, it's like walking into "enemy territory." Who knows what we'll encounter on the road ahead? Loneliness, wrinkles, stiff joints, indigestion, memory loss? We envision lugging a suitcase full of pills instead of party dresses, and trying to jump-start a mind that operates on only two cylinders, if and when it goes into gear.

My friend Edna defied all those stereotypes of "old." When we met, I was twenty and she was eighty. She lived alone in a three-room house two blocks from the college campus where I was a student. One of my greatest delights that year was visiting Edna. Her daughter, Marian, and I sang together in the church choir. One Sunday after the service, she invited a group of students to lunch, then to her mother's home. The idea of eating at the City Café held much more appeal than dorm dining, so there was a resounding *yes* from all of us. I thought the meal would be the highlight of that invitation, but I was wrong. It was Edna, the youngest old person I've ever known.

When we approached the little clapboard house in which Edna lived, I loved it immediately. There were flowers in abundance — all over the yard as well as in window boxes at every window. Classical music filled the air, along with the aroma of fresh baking bread. I wanted to take in everything as quickly as possible for fear it would be over too soon.

Edna, a sprightly, animated little woman, greeted Marian warmly, and when she was introduced to each of us, she curtsied and smiled. "Welcome to my house . . . how about a cup of tea?" I could hardly believe my eyes . . . ears . . . nose. Humming along with the music, Edna went into the kitchen while I became the roaming observer of her domain.

Books were everywhere . . . on shelves, the floor, the kitchen counter, the chairs, the bed. It was obvious she was either reading fifty of them or simply liked the pleasure of their company, so she surrounded herself with them, like good friends. Mesmerized, I asked something profound like, "You enjoy reading, Edna?"

"Oh, yes, I love it. I'll never have enough time to read all I want, but I'm making a dent in my list. Some of these books I've had all my life. They're old and weathered . . . like me," she said laughingly, "but I can't ever throw them away. I can't even put them in a box. And I'm always adding new ones."

Edna did all her own cooking, housework, gardening, laundry, shopping — and seemingly loved every minute of it. That was the first of numerous times I went to see her. I finally didn't even drum up an excuse for showing up on Sundays. I just liked Edna and the way she lived, and I wanted to be with her, learn from her, memorize how to be at any age.

She used to say little throwaways like, "While I'm making jam, I'm writing poetry in my head." Or "Planting flowers the other day, I worked on memorizing the first six Psalms." Or "I was standing at my kitchen window last week, when it hit me . . . *I think I'll paint the bathroom . . .* so I did." Or "I ran across a French word today while I was reading. Had to look it up so I could keep going."

What was Edna's secret? I've tried to figure it out, but have come to the conclusion that there wasn't one. She simply lived, and lived simply, every day . . . all the time. She integrated the whole of her life into everything she did, savoring her moments, counting her blessings, trying new things. Edna was Tasha Tudor, before her time.

If you want to have a life like that when you're eighty, you'd better start now. Here's what I recommend:

1. Stay spiritually centered with the Lord as your prime mover.
2. Learn something new every day and keep experimenting to make it better.
3. Wear your inside person outside, being who you really are.
4. Realize that tranquility is your greatest source of beauty.
5. Remember God's mercies are new every morning . . . and *that* is grace.

However many years a man may live, let him enjoy them all.

ECCLESIASTES 11:8

Guatemala Gals

I have to say I am *impressed* with World Vision. It's an international Christian relief agency that helps the poor all over the world by meeting needs in emergencies, development, training, and education. Because World Vision is in partnership with Women of Faith, we have an opportunity to see firsthand the work they're doing and to be actively engaged in their outreach.

One such occasion occurred in January 1999 when several of us flew to Guatemala to participate in their child sponsorship program. I have to admit, I was a little nervous before going. I was asked to sign a form disavowing World Vision from almost anything that could happen to me — injury, damage to my person or property, acts of terrorism, violence, kidnapping, hostage-taking. Little things like that! But I'm an adventurer at heart so I thought, *why not?* I signed, packed my bag, and headed for Central America.

Guatemala is a beautiful country. From my hotel window I could see two volcanoes (one was active with smoke billowing out). *Please!* There are bustling cities, colorful villages, jungles, highlands, lakes, and people with flawless brown skin and ready smiles. But there's a lot of sorrow behind all this beauty. Because the poverty level is high and incomes low, young Guatemalan girls have little chance of getting even the most basic education. It is in addressing this problem that World Vision finds one of its greatest challenges and highest achievements.

In spite of obvious deprivation, however, everywhere we went we saw happy individuals living lives of apparent fulfillment. One family had lost the roof of its house in Hurricane Mitch, yet they were so pleased we were there, nothing else mattered. The entire neighborhood turned out to watch us make tortillas. Patty-cake, patty-cake . . . it looked so simple but, as we discovered, it is a real art form. My tortillas were shaped just like Guatemala. Oh, well.

In one little hamlet, several miles from the capital city, World Vision has a very enterprising program where they make bank loans to Christian women, helping them improve their quality of life. Some of these women set up retail operations in their homes, others raise poultry or sell crafts.

When I met one of the women (a mother of two children) who had been given a loan to maintain a small chicken farm, I asked her which was harder — raising children or chickens. To my surprise, she said, "They're the same . . . each demands tenderness and responsibility. If you aren't careful to meet their needs, the baby chicks will die. It's the same with children."

What a great answer! I thought she'd say, "Oh, children, of course," but she didn't. She understood commitment — and the hard relentless work of tending to the needs of those in your care. I loved her reply. No nonsense. No phony philosophical platitudes. Real life.

Since then, I've had time to reflect on our visit to Guatemala, and I've realized that there was a time when

I might have seen people with little of this world's goods, eking out an existence or struggling to make ends meet, and thought, *There but for the grace of God go I.* In fact, I've said that many times. But no more. What that statement reveals is an attitude of, *I'm the recipient of more grace than they are. Look at what I have! God's been better to me than he has been to them.* That is simply not true. In fact, it's a very distorted view of grace.

Sometimes we have the mistaken idea that God loves and blesses us more if we look, live, or behave a certain way. If our lives are tidier, he's happier. If we are "successful" in the world's eyes, he's relieved. If we become cultured or erudite, he feels better about us. We assume God prefers designer clothes and custom homes. We presume he's pleased with fancy careers and technological advances. But in God's economy, grace doesn't work like that. God places *no* emphasis on externals. He looks at our hearts, and he blesses us from the inside out. His goodness is available to *all.*

Those Guatemala gals are wonderful reminders that God's grace is limitless. It's not dependent on anything we've done—or have. God gives us himself, in the person of Jesus Christ, and he does it whether we live in a New York City penthouse or under a thatched roof at the foot of a volcano. He loves us infinitely, with extravagant grace!

Praise the LORD. Give thanks to the LORD, for he is good; his love endures forever. Who can proclaim the mighty acts of the LORD or fully declare his praise?

PSALM 106:1–2

Gone Fishing

In my opinion, legalism is the greatest heresy of Christianity.
BILL BRIGHT

The sign GONE FISHING was a common sight on the door of my granddaddy's office. He had a successful insurance business in a small Texas town. But on certain occasions, nothing was more satisfying or more important to him than closing shop and heading toward the Gulf, rod and reel in hand. When he got word that the tide was in and the fish were biting, hardly anything could keep Granddaddy from the fine art of angling. In this field, he was a pro.

Not only was my grandfather into the sport of fishing, but my dad, a couple of uncles, some cousins, a brother, and even I loved to "reel 'em in and fry 'em whole." As a child I enjoyed these family outings, which at times occurred on a weekend, causing me to miss Sunday school and church. I rarely missed Sunday services, but a fishing trip with kith and kin was an excuse sanctioned by my parents. After all, I wasn't just playing hooky. I was doing something important.

My Sunday school teacher, Mrs. Borden (as in Lizzie) was a rather tight-jawed, strict, corseted woman in her sixties whose goal in life was to have perfect attendance week after week among her fledgling students. No excuse for being absent was acceptable. I rather hated her. Every

Sunday I spent class time dreaming up ways to blow up her car. With her in it.

One unforgettable morning after I'd been absent the week before because of a family fishing trip, Mrs. Borden quizzed me in front of the entire class. "Where were you last Sunday, Lovell Lucille?" (I know ... it's a family name.)

Frightened of public ridicule but not wanting to lie, I whispered, "I went fishing with my family."

"You what? Speak up so we can all hear you."

"I went fishing. We all went ... my granddaddy, mother, daddy, and two brothers."

"Well, now." Mrs. Borden smiled malevolently. "Do you think God can bless you when you aren't in his house on Sunday?"

I didn't know how to respond, so I just sat there, feeling sheepish and terribly embarrassed. Later I wished I'd said, "Of course she can, Axe-face." But I didn't think of it at the time.

Without apology, Mrs. Borden's eyes moved past me and on to the next student who had been absent the previous Sunday. He was openly questioned and criticized just as I had been.

I don't know what ever happened to Mrs. Borden (although I have a suspicion as to her present whereabouts), but I'll never forget that blatant display of legalism in her classroom. I've thought back on it many times, always with anguish for the indelible black smudge it left on my young soul.

You see, what legalism does is cling to the unbending letter of some artificial law at the expense of liberty in God's grace. It binds the Christian to performance and conformity. It kills the spirit. It robs one of the freedom there is in a relationship with Christ, thus forcing a particular behavioral code to be one's standard for living. What a shame!

Jesus Christ never taught that one person should tell another what to do, where to go, how to live. In fact, he reserved his harshest comments for those who tried. ("Whitewashed tombs" was his term for these know-it-alls!) Jesus said, "Follow me." He never instructed us to follow each other's rules. He never gave anyone control over another. His desire is that his Word and his Spirit be our guides for life. Being a follower of Jesus Christ means becoming more and more like him—letting his Spirit transform us into all we were created to be. That happens, dear friend, from the inside out.

Unfortunately, there will always be Mrs. Bordens in the world, ready to pounce on anything that smacks of grace and freedom. They'll be standing in the wings of your life, waiting to make their entrance with demands, curfews, criticism, and rules. They're always close at hand, wanting to squelch the passion and pleasure of knowing the Savior. Don't let them. And, more importantly, don't be one! As a follower of Christ you have the unique opportunity every day to demonstrate and celebrate his grace.

I love Jesus Christ today in large part because of the gracious godly influence of my granddaddy who took me fishing—sometimes on Sundays.

It is for freedom that Christ has set us free. Stand firm, then, and do not let yourselves be burdened again by a yoke of slavery.

GALATIANS 5:1

My Dependable Love

There are few words as disturbing as "terrorist," especially when you think you're sitting across the aisle from one.

I had boarded in New York for a flight to Miami and was happily seated in 14F, already into a fascinating book and cup of coffee, when I noticed the dude with the earphones. He was across the aisle, one row ahead, and not only indifferent to the request of the flight attendant to turn down the radio strapped to his waist, but every swig of beer was timed to the drumbeats of the music. His hair was actually blowing away from his face. Whoa!

We taxied back from the gate, and I have to admit everybody nearby began exchanging suspicious glances except the scrawny little dirty guy in 13B who had his eyes closed, feeling no pain. His five-o'clock shadow told me he either got up too late to shave or had blunted his razor while slitting his lover's throat less than an hour before. I chose the latter conclusion.

We were airborne when a second flight attendant tried to coax Hairy Dicer into turning down his radio, to no avail. He absolutely refused to obey, so life went on as normal in our little doomed ship of fools. The meal was offered and Harry refused that. He asked for a beer, gulping it as the rest of us ate. He requested a second beer and was given one. Huh? By now the questioning glances had become outright, downright staring.

At this very moment (about forty minutes into the flight), when we were sure our guy was going to pull out a grenade and blow us out of the sky, the head flight attendant, a tall, pretty blond woman with a calm, wide smile, walked up to terrorist Harry and said, "Sir, may I suggest you kindly lower your earphones? I'd like to ask you something."

Disarmed and struck dumb, he actually did so as every book and newspaper for miles around dropped to our laps with a pronounced thud. We watched and listened to this mesmerizing exchange:

"May I offer you something to eat? I realize you've had nothing but beer since you got on the plane. Surely you must be hungry."

"Do we go over water?"

"I beg your pardon?"

"Do we go over water . . . does this plane fly over the water?"

In calm assurance the attendant replied, "Yes, we do. For about 100 miles we are over the outer shoreline of the Atlantic Ocean."

"Are there life preservers on this plane?"

"Yes, they're under each seat." She smiled, looking straight at him.

Of course there are life preservers on this plane you moron you would have known that if you'd had the brains and thoughtfulness to lower your idiotic earphones and listen in the first place but you were too into your beer and stupidity to think of anybody else but yourself . . .

I digress.

"I'd like you to demonstrate one for me," said the terrorist.

At this his new friend asked him to stand, and with the greatest of ease and composure, she took the life jacket from under his seat, pulled it out of its sheath, put it on, and blew it up. All the while she talked with complete coolheadedness, explaining what to do if it was ever needed in an emergency situation.

"Would you like to try it on, sir?" she asked.

(Let me just interject, you could have heard a pin drop on that plane, even over the roar of the engines. All eyes, hearts, minds, and stomachs were riveted on this unequally yoked pair standing in the aisle. I just knew this was truly my final hour.)

Then it happened. The man with the radio, full of beer and bravado, replied, "No, thank you . . . that won't be necessary. I see how it works. I know you won't believe this, but I have never ever flown before. Never been in a plane or near a plane in my life, and I'm scared to death. I just wanted to know how these things work in case we crash."

WHAT??? Is that it? Is that all??? Good grief one of your victims would have been glad to hold your hand you jerk why didn't you just say I'M SCARED and act normal like the rest of us?

"I understand," responded our heroine. "Fear is a very natural emotion. A lot of people are afraid to fly. Why don't you gather up your things, come to the back of the plane with me, and we'll visit while you eat dinner?" And off they went.

Although this episode happened years ago, I've never forgotten it. Never will. I know nothing about that flight attendant. I don't even remember her name. But because of her kind, courageous behavior to a rude and defiant individual, she has impressed me for life. I think of her sometimes when I'm facing a scary-looking stranger. She demonstrated fearless love in a precarious situation. She didn't know any more about the man on the plane than we did, but she was in charge, so she took charge. Lovingly.

I believe this is one of the hardest, most challenging ways to express love. It is for me. It calls for courage I just don't have. It's built on an inner strength and boldness that is hidden somewhere inside, coming to the surface only in the most uncommon hour. The testing hour. And here's why it works:

> You've been a safe place for me, a good place to hide.
> Strong God, I'm watching you do it, I can always
>   count on you—
> God, my dependable love.

PSALM 59:16–17 MSG

That's it . . . those last four words: *God, my dependable love*. You don't have to crank out that kind of love. It's of God. It *is* God. That's why it's fearless.

True courage is cool and calm, not intense or proud. It's accepting difficult or disagreeable facts with peace and poise.

How Do You Spell Love?

I heard a little story recently that brought me pause. When a woman arrived at heaven's gates after succumbing to a long illness, she peeked in and saw people she'd known on earth seated at a beautiful banquet table, enjoying a sumptuous meal. She was amazed and thrilled.

Saint Peter showed up to greet her. "We've been waiting for you," he said. "It's good to see you."

"Thank you!" the woman replied. "How do I get into that banquet? It looks wonderful. I'd love to be with my old friends."

Saint Peter told her that she would have to spell a word correctly.

Having been a spelling bee winner as a child, she felt pretty confident when she asked, "Which word?"

"Love," Saint Peter replied.

She correctly spelled the simple word and was ushered right into the banquet hall.

About six months later Saint Peter asked the woman to mind the gates while he ran an errand. During this time her husband arrived at the pearly gates.

"Well, I'm surprised to see you," the woman said, smiling. "How have you been since I died?"

"Oh, I've been great," he enthused. He recounted how he'd married the beautiful young nurse who took care of his wife when she was sick. He'd won the lottery, sold the little house they'd lived in all their married life, and bought a big mansion across town. He bought a brand-new Cadillac and traveled around the world with his new wife. Unfortunately, all the fun was cut short by the water ski that plunked him in the head that afternoon while he was vacationing in the Bahamas.

"So, here I am," he said. "How do I get in there? The food looks great!"

"You have to spell a word," his old wife replied.

"Which word?"

"Czechoslovakia."

Consider this silly little story for a minute, because there's a very important lesson to be learned. It's awfully hard not to retaliate when we've been hurt or rejected or maligned, isn't it? Wanting to get even is one of the worst battles we all fight. Many people sit around obsessing about ways to get back at somebody. They *love* to get even. But how can the desire to *love* and *get even* live in the same heart at the same moment? It's an oxymoron.

We all know the thought of getting even isn't new. Two thousand years before the birth of Christ the prophet Jeremiah said, "The heart is deceitful above all things and beyond cure. Who can understand it?" (Jer. 17:9). The heart will always have the capacity for leaning in an evil direction, even after we have embraced Christ as our Savior and Lord.

So it's certainly a good thing that our entrance into heaven isn't dependent on the correct spelling of a word! Even the word *love,* since no human being can ever live that one out right. Getting into heaven isn't dependent on our doing *anything* correctly, praise God! Redemption rests on the finished work of Christ on the cross.

When Jesus died, he did so for you and me and our "deceitful" hearts that can never get it right. The Bible says the penalty for not getting it right according to God's perfect standard is death, and Christ paid that penalty *for us*. The other great news is that as a result of his Spirit dwelling in us through salvation, we experience divine power to live a life that is above getting even, demanding our "rights," and hurting other people. Christ's death and resurrection empower us to do what we can't muster up in ourselves. Christ sees to it that we can enjoy a love relationship with him today and for all eternity. We can get into heaven with no spelling bee—no contest!

Unfortunately, this does not mean our lives on earth will be easy and without self-centered feelings and desires. As the apostle Paul so clearly states, there is still a natural desire in us to do what is wrong. "I know that nothing good lives in me, that is, in my sinful nature. For I have the desire to do what is good, but I cannot carry it out. For what I do is not the good I want to do; no, the evil I do not want to do—this I keep on doing" (Rom. 7:18–19).

How frustrating! As long as we're alive, that tension is not going to go away. But let me suggest a couple of practical things that help me cope with my own desires to do wrong or "get even" at the expense of someone I'm called to love. When I'm able to do this, it really works.

Keep your mouth closed. Every time you want to gossip or speak evil of someone or set the record straight because you've been wronged, stuff a sock in your mouth if you have to. Vengeance belongs to the Lord, and he is fighting for you. Leave the battle to him.

Keep your sin confessed. When sin comes in (and it will), or when you want to get even (and you will), immediately confess that to God. He loves you with a stubborn love that never gives up on you, and he promises to help you in your areas of weakness. The power to overcome is in him, not in you.

Unlike our human love that often goes off course, digging in its heels in righteous indignation, the love of God is righteously stubborn. He didn't die for us for nothing. It was the mercy of the Father that sent the Son to die. Now that's an oxymoron you can sink your teeth into. It's the very essence of how love is correctly spelled.

Haulin' Freedom

Every place has its pitfalls and absurdities,
just as each has its opportunities and measures of grace.
DANIEL TAYLOR

If there ever was a place that lends itself to one's expression of autonomy, it's the Los Angeles freeway system. I don't know if it's because so many of the freeways lead to Hollywood and folks think there might be a talent scout in their lane looking for the next Thelma and Louise, or because O. J. Simpson gained such notoriety racing north on the 405 in search of his own freedom. There's just something about the word *freeway* that makes people think it's exactly that: their way to freedom.

During my twenty-five years in California, I've seen it all: Daredevil pedestrians running across the freeway at rush hour. Some poor soul trying to jump off an overpass. Motorcyclists weaving at breakneck speed between moving vehicles. Two motorists parked on the shoulder throwing rocks at one another's cars. I've witnessed creative hand gestures, men shaving, women applying mascara, violent arguments, speed races, road rage, romance, and other acts of recklessness. (Did I ever tell you about the time I saw a clown in the driver's seat?)

Undoubtedly, the most ingenious expression of "freeway freedom" I ever saw was on a summer afternoon. I don't remember the temperature, but it was hot and getting hotter! Nobody wants to be anywhere on a day like that, much less in traffic. It was ghastly.

There I was, driving along, when suddenly out of my peripheral vision I spotted something I could not believe. In the middle lane was a pickup truck, going about 50 mph, with a makeshift swimming pool rigged up in the bed of the truck. Three children were having the time of their lives, yelling, splashing water, diving in, horsing around with rubber toys. I will have to say it looked so inviting I considered joining them. I didn't, of course, but I did join all the other motorists in my lane as we created what we refer to in California as "gawker's block" — slow down and stare.

The driver of this moving circus animatedly chatted with his passenger in the cab as they raced blithely along. Music was blasting out the windows, and everybody was happy as a clam. The driver was oblivious to the stir he was causing, and certainly was unaware he was about to be in a heap of trouble for endangering the lives of those in his pickup!

It wasn't until the next morning when I opened the newspaper that I learned what finally happened. There was a photo of this very truck, wet children, and embarrassed driver as a police officer was handing him a traffic citation for breaking the law. The short article quoted the driver as saying, "It was so hot and the kids were having so much fun, I just hated to stop them."

Everybody in that truck thought they were free to do whatever they wanted — if they were thinking at all. Their perspective reminded me of the line Debbie Boone sings in "You Light Up My Life": "How can it be wrong when it feels so right?" Haven't we all thought that at times? During the sixties, there was strong emphasis on expressing your freedom no matter what: let your hair grow, burn your bra and your draft card, sleep in the grass, make love not war, cry freedom—from parental rule, regimentation, traditions, the control of others. And yet, is this really freedom?

Well, this I know: Freedom is not taking the law into our own hands. It's not putting someone else at risk. It's not doing what we please simply because it feels "good" or "right." If we want to truly enjoy freedom, we need to realize that our liberty was bought at an exorbitant price and with it comes an enormous responsibility. It's based on grace, found in the life, death, and resurrection of Jesus Christ. And it's expressed in service, not sanction. In giving, not getting. In liberty, not license. It's not doing what we please, it's pleasing God in what we do. That's where real freedom lies.

The book of Galatians teaches that we've been set free to serve the Savior joyfully, not to serve the law grudgingly. Our greatest way to freedom is obeying and serving Jesus Christ. Now, that's a truth worth haulin' down the freeway.

Don't you know that when you offer yourselves to someone to obey him as slaves, you are slaves to the one whom you obey—whether you are slaves to sin, which leads to death, or to obedience, which leads to righteousness?

ROMANS 6:16

xoxo DP

I hate forwarded e-mail. It's absolutely maddening to me, and while I'd like to be passive about it, I'm not. If you're inclined to send me a cute joke or heart-wrenching story, a perky prayer or silly song, an irresistible piece of wit or wisdom, please . . . don't do it. It drives me crazy.

One day I came home from a long trip and there in my in-box were forty-six forwarded messages . . . from the same person. *Please.* Even if you want to tell me I'm among the five recipients who just won a box of Snickers waiting to be picked up next door, don't. Even if you're informing me that an airplane has been reserved to fly me to my favorite place in the world if I will just read this message, don't. Even if you have suggestions for the greatest manuscript under my name that will bring me a fortune if I will only click onto something.com, don't. Don't ever, ever forward me anything.

However, let me tell you what I do like in e-mail. I like to get messages that are sweet, kind, encouraging, informative . . . and not everlastingly long. I like words from the heart. I like original thoughts. I like information and Scriptures from an understanding, sympathetic friend that will help me on my way in life. And I like clever notes from people who have a way with words. Words that snap and tickle and assure and thrill me to the bone. I like e-mail from Sheila and Annie and Mary and Steve and Traci. They stir my mental "pot" and make me think. They stimulate my imagination and make me laugh. And most of all, they love me. Therefore, they don't ever, ever forward anything to me. That is almost my favorite thing about their cyber correspondence — *no forwarded mail.*

But my classic correspondent, who really has no peers, is Debra Petersen. She fills all the bills. Not only does she e-mail me warm, wonderful personal notes every day from her home in Miami (never anything forwarded), but she also sends me all kinds of snail mail. Hardly a day goes by that I don't find in my mailbox a note or little package from her, housed in a colorful envelope, with my name in big, scrawly, neon writing in her own hand. And I haven't even gotten to the most fun part. Inside that envelope there is apt to be just about anything that speaks of love . . . a cassette tape to encourage me, a card especially chosen just to lift my spirits, a torn-out magazine page with a Post-It note, "I love this" or "Reminds me of you" or "I can just see you in this so I ordered it for you."

Debbie does this kind of thing for countless people, not just me. She keeps the U.S. Postal Service in business. And UPS and FedEx too. Literally. In fact, she told me she has to *stop herself* from sending things to people she loves and those she wants to help. "I love mailing little notes and packages," she says, "because it's like having a visit with people I don't see very often." Can you beat that? She has a room called "the factory" in her small apartment where her multitude of correspondence is handled. (Maybe she has that line from *The Mask* nailed up in there too — "Somebody stop me!")

Let me just wax a minute more about my friend Debbie. She works for Campus Crusade for Christ, but if you've ever been to a Women of Faith conference or one of the "Intensive" meetings on the Friday afternoon before each conference, you've seen her because she's the emcee for those events. It's not as though the girl has nothing to do but haunt the post office. She is wildly busy with a full life of ministry and outreach. It never stops. There are parties and parades and programs for everybody she knows. With personal invitations.

Debra Petersen takes her time with each person she touches. There's the initial encounter of a smile, warm words, and an understanding heart. Then there's the follow-up of a note or Scripture. Ultimately, you receive photos she's taken when she was with you, little presents, maybe candy or books or fresh-baked bread. As she says, "I send anything I think will encourage the person who gets it." Wow! What a giver of love in tiny, daily snippets. Because most people don't get much cheerful e-mail or snail mail, Debbie makes up for the whole world. From her heart. A heart that is sold out to being a light in a dark place. Debbie lavishes love in minutes and seconds and nanoseconds. xoxoDP. How often have I seen that trademark signature at the bottom of one of her notes?

Wanna know how to get on Debbie's correspondence list? I think the truth is you just have to meet her. That seems to be enough. I have no idea how nor why God blessed me with the extravagant attention of this unique friend. I'm truly rich from her simple giving. What Deb does without even knowing it is make me want to be more of a lavish giver myself, in small but consistent ways. She emulates the beauty and reward of doing to others what you want done to you.

The English poet Shelley said, "Familiar acts are beautiful through love," and Debbie lives the truth of that message. She has it engraved across the doorposts of her life, and it is the genuine experience for everybody who enters.

Debbie simply loves lavishly and has made the familiar act of correspondence a fine art to lift the hearts of literally hundreds of people. I'm just one of the lucky ones.

I'm going to alter my initial request just this once and close with a personal suggestion to you: you may forward this devotional to anybody you want. xoxoLS.

Thoreau once wrote in his journal, "There is no remedy for love but to love more." Send that in your next e-mail.

Nothin' Says Lovin' Like Somethin' from the Oven

I love to cook. Well, maybe not *love,* but strongly like. There's something about creating wonderful dishes in the kitchen that makes me feel alive. I'm enhancing my health. I'm saving money. I'm aiding the war effort. You get the picture. In the words of Martha Stewart, cooking is "a good thing."

I don't pretend to be as skilled as my two gourmet friends Ruth or Kurt, but I make a mean soufflé. Don't ever ask me to make bread, though. I did that once for the first and last time. It was such a failure I'm now writing a book entitled *One Loaf, That's All I Knead.* My worst moment in the kitchen.

Oh, and then there's that time Daddy and I made a pecan pie. Long after Mother died (who was fabulous with pies . . . and bread, I might add), I said to my dad, "Let's make a pecan pie. It's a beautiful fall day and we'll pool our resources and whip out the world's prettiest pie . . . it'll be fun." He loved the idea, shelled the pecans . . . and I made the crust.

Oh. My. Gosh. Have you ever *made crust?* Let me give you a word of advice: don't. It's an impossible task. I thought defrosting a refrigerator was tough, or cleaning the oven, but making, baking, scraping crust is much, much worse. I must have either left something out or put something in that caused me to wind up with a small plate of cement. When that pie (which actually looked pretty good upon completion) came out of the oven and we tried to cut it, both Daddy and I used a chisel, literally, to remove it from the pan. Not even one pecan budged. Nada.

But . . . you know what I totally enjoyed about that pie? The fun we had making it! The whole idea of *me and Daddy* trying to follow in Mother's footsteps was outlandish in the first place. We laughed our heads off, sang, horsed around. Who cares if our masterpiece looked like a Frisbee?

The well-known, incomparable chef Wolfgang Puck once said, "Cooking is my *kinder spiel* — my child's play. You can make it yours too. And while you're cooking, don't forget to share and laugh. Laugh a great deal, and with much love — it enhances the flavor of food."

Ain't it the truth? Lovin' from the oven, right there.

Both Ruth and Kurt have told me that a full meal can be made effectively in twenty minutes, and who am I to doubt them? I've eaten at each of their tables many times and reveled in the delicious food. But the sweetest thing about being their guest is observing the joy with which they cook and entertain. Nothing is too hard and nobody is in the way. Everybody wants to be in the kitchen. That's where all the creativity takes place, the best laughs, the most extraordinary moments. As guests, we may not want to do the cooking, but we want to watch the experts.

In Wolfgang Puck's cookbook *Modern French Cooking,* he talks about the joy he finds in cooking and the men and women who influenced him in his culinary career — his beloved grandmother, famous French chefs, restaurant owners. He tells about the poetic approach they had toward the fine art of preparing a meal, the confidence they poured into him, and the freedom they gave him to grow and make mistakes. He refers to the *love* they had for cooking and for their guests.

I realize most of us who cook are doing so for a family. Everybody's hungry and eager for a good meal; obviously that atmosphere has the potential to create tension. But, trust me on this, when the meal is finished and the table is clear, rare is the person who's going to ponder the recipe used or why the dishes didn't match. More likely they're going to remember conversations, laughter, zany moments, and the way they were treated.

What is the legacy you are leaving through the domain of your kitchen? Will people remember they were encouraged in that room, or criticized? Will they recall the fun or the fights? Will they think of sharing recipes and culinary efforts with good humor or one-upmanship? We, as women, have a splendid opportunity to impart the love of Christ from a simple dining table or kitchen stove. It doesn't take a lot — just remembering our *kinder spiel* — our "child's play."

I asked Marilyn one Christmas to give me her favorite recipe. We had been working together, having a great time as we fixed dinner. Without the slightest hesitation she said, "Okay, write this down" — and I did.

Marilyn's Favorite Recipe for Smooth and Satiny Brown Gravy

4 c. flour
1 c. fruit cocktail (with liquid)
1 T. white pepper
1 tsp. nutmeg
3 T. salt
1 c. arrowroot

2 tsp. cinnamon
1 c. raisins

Take a 5-lb. mallet, place in palm of right hand. Methodically coerce lumps into satiny submission. Allow one hour for smooth and satiny effect. May be made ahead of time and stored until the return of Christ. Serve in silver, which enhances flavor. Serves 23 guests, give or take 12. (Aunt Rebecca wanly commented after four bites: "Something's amiss, but . . ." — after which she slipped quietly into a coma.)

I cannot tell you how I *love, love, love* that outlandish recipe. It's mine forever and I've read it a thousand times. I jotted it in my journal in 1987. When I'm fed up with problems and people and life, I whip it out and read it again. I may even make that gravy someday and not only slip into a coma but die a happy woman.

Pick up a copy of Sophia Loren's cookbook, *Recipes and Memories.* It's not only full of great-looking food but a bushel of love and affection as well.

God's Greatest Compliments

I was lying in bed early this morning when I thought of a way to begin this devotional. For several weeks I've been writing, trying to finish my chapters, so just as I awakened I asked the Lord to help me be creative. Then it hit me. How 'bout this for an opening paragraph?

"Draw, you lily-livered, life-suckin' maggot," she said as she faced her opponent at the far end of the bar. "If you think you're leavin' this town with my man, you're crazy. I said—DRAW."

Ummm . . . okay. That's different. Eye-catching. A creative way to start a Christian devotional. *Are you sure, Lord? Did I hear that right?* I wasn't sure where the story line would go from there, but I tore out of bed, raced to the computer, booted up, and started writing. Soon I realized that this was a fresh, fun answer to my prayer . . . a great way to begin the day.

A little while later, with a smile on my face and spring in my step, I marched triumphantly into the kitchen, put on the coffee, and something equally refreshing happened. I looked at the *Joyful Journey* flip calendar on my counter, and it so happened that the quote for the day was something I had written:

> Find a new way to greet the day. Try a new way to drive to work—even if it's longer. Don't let the beaten path you travel daily beat you down too.

Oh my. How many times I've asked God for something specific, and he's dropped it in my lap; but because it didn't look like what I thought it should, I turned it down. *Forget that, Lord,* I say. *You've gotta be kidding.* God doesn't kid. He's the master of creativity, if I just trust him on that. So this morning I'm back at the drawing board, and I'm gonna *draw.*

I've discovered that life is so much easier when I take everything as a compliment from God. Every innovative idea, every unexpected circumstance, every outlandish twist along my path. The compliments I'm referring to are wrapped up in the mystery of becoming seasoned in the Lord as we grow more intimately acquainted with him, as we learn to see and hear past what is happening on the surface of our lives.

I learned this lesson the hard way. In 1982 I wrote my first book and was out of my head with joy about being The New Author on the block. I wrote constantly, talked about my writing, read chapters to everybody who slowed down long enough to listen, discussed ideas for the book with my editor and friends, traveled to the publishing house to meet the staff, kept a notebook about the progress I made. In short, I became a royal pain in the neck.

One day as I was waxing on and on with one of my dear friends, she lovingly told me that I was becoming a bore with all this book stuff. I was dominating dinner parties and weekends and was totally self-absorbed. Nobody else had the courage to point this out, but to save me from myself, she did.

I hated that revelation. It hurt me to hear those truthful words from a person I so loved. But, as I reasoned through her comments in the days ahead, I realized she was absolutely right. Then I wanted to retreat and never see those other friends again, I was so embarrassed by my self-centered behavior.

But as the weeks and months passed, and as I prayed about how I'd behaved and how to change, the Lord showed me something very helpful in James 1:2–5 (TLB). I had read it before, but that day it stuck.

> Is your life full of difficulties and temptations? Then be happy, for when the way is rough, your patience has a chance to grow. So let it grow, and don't try to squirm out of your problems. For when your patience is finally in full bloom, then you will be ready for anything, strong in character, full and complete. If you want to know what God wants you to do, ask him, and he will gladly tell you, for he is always ready to give a bountiful supply of wisdom to all who ask him.

You see, *nothing* in our lives is wasted. Not one thing that happens is without worth somewhere down the road. But we often miss it because we "travel the beaten path" and fail to open our eyes to the outlandish ways God wants to speak to us and love us and change us. We don't recognize the value in celebrating the strange twists, the difficulties, the so-called failures, when we really should ... and could. We consider our flops or hard times a defeat, but in reality they are God's greatest compliments. They're transforming love gifts from a gracious heavenly Father.

There's an account of this very point in *Say Please, Say Thank You* by Donald McCullough. The Ore-Ida frozen potato company celebrates anniversaries of failure. (They're the folks who make frozen cauliflower, broccoli, mushrooms, French fries, etc., and they're famous for innovative, creative ideas.) But what do they do when one of those ideas bombs? Do they blame or fire some-body? No, they throw a party! Literally. A cannon is fired and everybody stops work to commemorate the "perfect failure." Together they rejoice in what they've learned. They talk about what will not work, reveling in the fact that no more time, energy, or money has to be spent on a thankless project. They "celebrate their freedom to go on."

I'm not advocating a Pollyanna approach to life. That's totally unrealistic. We all go through terrible times of anx-iety and loss—very real pain that takes time to go away, if it ever does. But there's a big difference between that and crawling under the house when things don't go our way or when our path takes what appears to be a too-outlandish turn.

If you wake up tomorrow with a thought that seems just a little bit crazy, or if a loved one brings your ego down to earth with a thud, take heart. It's God's compli-mentary gift to remind you who's in charge, who gives you freedom to go on . . . and who loves you with an out-landish love.

Of all powers, love is the most powerful because it alone can conquer that final and most impregnable stronghold which is the human heart.

FREDERICK BUECHNER

Plotting for Love

In the early spring of 1966 I went to Berlin for the first time. What an amazing, beautiful city! Even though it was marked by mounds of rubble and devastation from World War II, there were many things I remember with love: the Dahlem Museum, Charlottenberg Palace, Kennedy Platz, Kongress Hall, the Kurfurstendamm Strasse, the Kaiser Wilhelm church. One could easily see the architectural beauty that was once the glory of Germany.

At the time I was traveling with a friend whose relatives lived there, and we had the good fortune to be guests in their home. They introduced their friends and treated us like queens.

I recall an experience during the last afternoon of our visit that touched me deeply. We were riding in their car as they pointed out various spots of interest: buildings, monuments, streets, churches, stores. We drove through a neighborhood of modest homes, all built by hand after the bombings. Attached to every dwelling was a tiny plot of ground, beautifully manicured and full of green plants. None of the plots could have been larger than forty square feet. I asked about them.

"Those are love plots," I was told. "After the war, each person who built here received one as part of their property. Everybody who owns a house cultivates that plot of ground however they want. Some plant trees, others flowers or vegetables. We call them 'love plots' because the soil is tilled not only with labor . . . but with love."

These lush little plots of ground struck me as more beautiful than any magnificent work of architecture I had seen. We were further told that the citizens of West Berlin were so devastated after the war that cultivating these tiny plots helped them come back to the center of what was important in their lives. They could plow and dig and hack and sow and plant and harvest to give life not only to what they were growing in the ground but to their souls as well. Somehow those forty-square-foot plots gave a sense of sanity and homeostasis to the people who had lost so much in the war. It gave them a start. A new beginning. A purpose.

Life is like that at times. We are overwhelmed by someone who has hurt us, smeared our name, slandered our reputation. We feel there is never going to be even the smallest spot in our heart where there can be a new beginning. But the human spirit is resilient. After the destruction and anguish, eventually there is some small movement within us toward rebuilding. There is the first outcropping of creative energy and advancement toward recovery.

It starts slowly, a small flicker of light in the darkness, just enough to illumine what is eating us up inside. We open our hearts a crack, the light comes in, and change begins. It rarely commences with one major, gargantuan leap. As C. S. Lewis says in *Mere Christianity,* "If we really want to learn how to forgive, perhaps we had better start with something easier than the Gestapo."

Don't set your aim too high. Start with just "forty square feet," cultivating and overturning one lifeless clod of ground at a time. Through slowly and intentionally tending our inner landscape, we find that God's power flows in to change and soften our spirit. In time we realize that the thing we hate, that which has been paralyzing us, is usually our own fear or pride rather than an external enemy.

I well remember an occasion in my own life when there was a breach in one of my relationships. So much bitterness had lodged in my heart that I thought the feeling of betrayal would never go away. In the words of Marilyn's grandson, I was "boilin' mad" inside and had even thought of revenge. But time passed, and I got sick of myself living in the darkness of that animosity. I began to pray, first tentatively, then with solid intention, about the burden I was carrying and the person who had hurt me.

Little by little the surface of my packed-down feelings cracked open. A shaft of light got in and illumined and brought to life a seed of hope. Eventually I picked up the phone and talked to the individual by whom I felt betrayed. I purposefully reached out, and healing and growth began.

I've learned that as I bury the pain of hatred, I am planting the seeds of forgiveness. Working with actual dirt in my garden somehow helps me concentrate on what is simple and basic. Essential. The source of life is there in my hands. All I have to do is put the seed in the ground and growth starts.

The same is true of the human heart. Change doesn't begin until I *do* something to start it. With that modicum of movement in the right direction, the Lord shines his warm light on the hard ground of my heart, and it softens. The writer of the letter to the Hebrews says, "Work at getting along with each other and with God. Otherwise you'll never get so much as a glimpse of God. Make sure no one gets left out of God's generosity. Keep a sharp eye out for weeds of bitter discontent. A thistle or two gone to seed can ruin a whole garden in no time" (Heb. 12:14–15 MSG).

When our lives have been broken in battle and embittered by betrayal, the only place to start getting better is with a small plot. Inch by inch the soil of our heart is tilled and pruned by the Savior. It is beyond human reasoning or power to forgive someone who took everything we had and reduced us to rubble. But God, *but GOD,* in his boundless love, will meet us right in that very place and start planting the seeds of hope and peace and strength and forgiveness . . . and we will come to life again. In the words of Henri Nouwen, "Love is an act of forgiveness in which evil is converted to good and destruction into creation."

The Berliners gave beauty to that which was ugly. They toiled together making gardens of green from mounds of rubble and ruin. Nobody said it was easy, but everybody said it was worth it.

Do some digging in the soil of your hearts and see what turns up. Make up your mind to let God plant some new seeds in the "plot" of your soul. And then grow.

The Fabric of Love

You wonder why some women never marry? There are, of course, many reasons, but one is that they never find Mr. Perfect. *Where is he?* They are looking for a guy the height of John Wayne, with the build of Schwarzeneggar, the looks of Omar Shariff, the wit of Dick Cavett, and the know-how of McGyver. He's out there somewhere, they just *know* it. But where?

Edna St. Vincent Millay wrote a tongue-in-cheek poem called *To the Not Impossible Him* where she confesses there is no way to know for sure you've met the right man unless you consider a good many . . . unless you travel the world and test the waters. I'm sure there's some truth to that.

My mom and dad had an almost perfect love match. The year Mother died they were just about to celebrate their fortieth wedding anniversary, and every year they were married was full of simple and intentional celebrations of their love and thoughtfulness to each other.

I was cleaning out a drawer a couple of mornings ago and ran across some of Mother's old jewelry; worthless stuff generally, but touching to me, nevertheless. In that batch of stuff was a compact with powder and rouge still in it, believe it or not. I saw it many times when I was growing up. Daddy gave it to her shortly after they married in 1931, and Mother told me he had mailed it from one of his trips with a note about how much he loved her.

On the little powder puffs he'd printed in big letters—EARL—so she would see his name and think of his love every time she opened that compact.

I love it when couples and friends do that kind of thing for one another. It says so much about their love, and it's often treasured for life. Just think, my mother carried that compact until she died in 1971, and every time she opened it, there was her husband's name, saying "I love you."

If I didn't love the single life so much, I might be looking for Mr. Perfect too. In fact, the closest ideal I've ever met with respect to my first-paragraph dreamboat is my longtime friend Kurt Ratican. He's handsome, bright, well-read, terribly witty, clever, and exceedingly kind. He's not . . . well . . . *perfect*. But close. And he does the same types of things my father did for my mother. He sends his love to me in unique ways all the time.

Among Kurt's many artistic talents is weaving, and he taught me to weave on a tiny wooden loom that was a Christmas gift from him in 1969. Included with the loom was a guidebook called *Simple Weaving*. It's full of his notes of instruction and encouragement. When I look at it, I think back on the day he gave me the loom and the sweet kindness that followed.

Because we lived in different states at the time (he in California and I in Texas), he told me he would "dress" the loom the first time if I'd let him take it home after our Christmas celebrations together. I was a novice so was thrilled at the prospect of his doing the hardest work. I knew nothing about heddles, raddles, bobbins, drums, cranks, or shuttles, and he knew *everything*. (Actually I knew about cranks, but that's another story.) I was one happy girl.

Kurt owns a very large loom and has woven many beautiful things for me through the years; but nothing of his design or thoughtfulness could have pleased me more than what I saw when I opened the box he sent back to me after the holidays. There sat the completely dressed loom with a portion of a geometric design already well on its way to completion. *Kurt's started a project,* I thought. *All right!* But just as I unwound the paper in which the gift was packed, I saw the best part: peeking out at me were the words *I love you* woven into the warp in red letters.

What a darling idea. I cut that piece of fabric off the loom, glued it to a small bar of wood, and hung it in my studio. I look at it every day, and did so again not five minutes ago. For over thirty years that tiny wall hanging has silently called out Kurt's love over and over, across the decades and across the miles.

Every one of us has little opportunities each day to intentionally weave love into somebody else's life. Maybe it's through a note in a school lunch box for your son or daughter. Maybe it's a short message scribbled in the dust on top of the dresser before you leave for work. It might be a bouquet of flowers to thank someone for a kindness. What about a smile to your neighbor, a song over the phone, a prayer on someone's behalf? Once when Kurt visited me, he hid twenty little love notes all over the place where I found them for weeks after he left. All but the one he swears he put in the oven.

The point is, don't sit around waiting for the big knock-your-socks-off opportunity to say "I love you." It's the "little things" that really make a difference in the lives of those you love. Mother Teresa once said, "We ourselves feel that what we are doing is just a drop in the ocean. But if that drop was not in the ocean, I think the ocean would be less because of that missing drop. I do not agree with the big way of doing things."

I want to make that simple heart attitude and intentional giving of myself a part of the fabric of my daily living. How about you?

I don't want to live — I want to love first, and live incidentally.

ZELDA FITZGERALD

ᵼ FAITH

Women of Faith partners with various Christian
organizations, including Zondervan,
Campus Crusade for Christ International,
Crossings Book Club, Integrity Music,
International Bible Society,
Partnerships, Inc., and World Vision
to provide spiritual resources for women.

For more information about Women of Faith
or to register for one of our nationwide conferences,
call 1-800-49-FAITH.

www.women-of-faith.com

Women of Faith Devotionals

Joy Breaks
Hardcover 0-310-21345-2

We Brake for Joy!
Hardcover 0-310-22042-4
Audio Pages® Abridged Cassettes 0-310-22434-9

OverJoyed!
Hardcover 0-310-22653-8
Audio Pages® Abridged Cassettes
0-310-22760-7

Extravagant Grace
Hardcover 0-310-23125-6
Audio Pages® Abridged
Cassettes 0-310-23126-4

Resources for Women of Faith℠

BOOKS/AUDIO

The Joyful Journey	Hardcover	0-310-21344-4
	Softcover	0-310-22155-2
	Audio Pages® Abridged Cassettes	0-310-21454-8
	Daybreak	0-310-97282-5
Bring Back the Joy	Hardcover	0-310-22023-8
	Softcover	0-310-22915-4
	Audio Pages® Abridged Cassettes	0-310-22222-2
Outrageous Joy	Hardcover	0-310-22648-1
	Audio Pages® Abridged Cassettes	0-310-22660-0

WOMEN OF FAITH BIBLE STUDY SERIES

Celebrating Friendship	0-310-21338-X
Discovering Your Spiritual Gifts	0-310-21340-1
Embracing Forgiveness	0-310-21341-X
Experiencing God's Presence	0-310-21343-6
Finding Joy	0-310-21336-3
Growing in Prayer	0-310-21335-5
Knowing God's Will	0-310-21339-8
Strengthening Your Faith	0-310-21337-1

WOMEN OF FAITH WOMEN OF THE BIBLE STUDY SERIES

Deborah: Daring to Be Different for God	0-310-22662-7
Esther: Becoming a Woman God Can Use	0-310-22663-5
Hannah: Entrusting Your Dreams to God	0-310-22667-8
Mary: Choosing the Joy of Obedience	0-310-22664-3
Ruth: Trusting That God Will Provide for You	0-310-22665-1
Sarah: Facing Life's Uncertainties with a Faithful God	0-310-22666-X

WOMEN OF FAITH Zondervan*Groupware*™

Capture the Joy	Video Curriculum Kit	0-310-23096-9
	Leader's Guide	0-310-23101-9
	Participant's Guide	0-310-23099-3

*Inspirio's innovative and elegant gift books
capture the joy and encouragement that is an integral part
of the Women of Faith^SM movement.*

Joy for a Woman's Soul
Promises to Refresh Your Spirit
ISBN: 0-310-97717-7

Grace for a Woman's Soul
Reflections to Renew Your Spirit
ISBN: 0-310-97996-X

**Hope for a
Woman's Soul**
*Meditations to
Energize Your
Spirit*
ISBN: 0-310-98010-0

Simple Gifts
*Unwrapping the Special
Moments of Everyday Life*
ISBN: 0-310-97811-4

Padded Hardcover
4 x 7
208 pages

*Verses from the New International Version of
the Bible have been collected into these topically arranged volumes
to inspire Women of Faith^SM on their spiritual journey.*

Prayers for a Woman of Faith^SM
ISBN: 0-310-97336-8

**Words of Wisdom
for a Woman of Faith^SM**
ISBN: 0-310-97390-2

**Promises of Joy
for a Woman of Faith^SM**
ISBN: 0-310-97389-9

**Words of Wisdom
for a Woman of Faith^SM**
ISBN: 0-310-97735-5

**Psalms and Proverbs
for a Woman of Faith^SM**
ISBN: 0-310-98092-5

**Promises of Love
for a Woman of Faith^SM**
ISBN: 0-310-98249-9

Hardcover
5-1/4 x 5-1/4
128 pages

We want to hear from you. Please send your comments about this book to us in care of the address below. Thank you.

ZONDERVAN™

GRAND RAPIDS, MICHIGAN 49530

www.zondervan.com